37 BLESSINGS OF GROWING UP AS A MISSIONARY KID

The Lord Saves Those Crushed in Spirit

37 BLESSINGS OF GROWING UP AS A MISSIONARY KID

The Lord Saves Those Crushed in Spirit

By
Carolyn Tubbs Van Valkenburg

37 Blessings
Growing Up As A Missionary Kid

ISBN-13: 978-1499179972

Printed in the United States of America
CreateSpace, Charleston, South Carolina

Author contact information:
blessings37@outlook.com

The front cover subtitle comes from the ESV
from Psalms 34:18

PREFACE

While reflecting on growing up as an MK, Carolyn Tubbs Van Valkenburg asks the "Why" questions.

This is the testimony of Carolyn's personal brokenness brought on by rejection and bullying and how God used this to cut off the rough edges of her life and to make her into a diamond sparkling for Jesus Christ. Her book gives answers to two questions: "Why does God allow suffering?" and "How may I have victory over rejection and bullying?"

Dedication

This book is dedicated to my dear
Father and Mother,
George and Martha Tubbs
who diligently made me obey
and taught me to fear God,
which means to be in awe of
and to be respectful of God.
This fear of God is the greatest gift
parents should endeavor
to give to their children!
I am eternally grateful
for my Mother and Father.

Special Thanks

My journey has been joined by so many other
MKs from other MK schools and other countries.
One of them for whom I am so very grateful
is one of my dearest and kindest of friends,
Brenda Ritchey, who has worked with me through
the process of publishing this book.

TABLE OF CONTENTS

Chapter 1
Leaving Home For Boarding School

There are absolutely no words to describe the horrifying feelings of grief as the day to leave for boarding school approached. I think gradually the shock turned into numbness. *Just don't think about it,* I'd tell myself.

This "sending your children away, hundreds of miles to live in a boarding school" was a result of the calling by God for my parents to bring the Bible's message to the people of Sayaboury, Laos, where we were the only white people.

In spite of the calling of God to my parents, as a child, I had no choice! Quite frankly, at that age I was horrified! I could not comprehend why I was leaving home to attend boarding school hundreds of miles away for four and a half months and then four and a half months again (totaling nine months out of the year). It was just something we had to do. Our denomination required it.

This brings me to my **first blessing** as an MK

(missionary kid), and that is learning at an early age to do something very heartbreaking and yet seeing that I could survive and survive well! Though I might have felt as if I was falling apart inside, outside God gave me grace to try to do my best by obeying my parents and my new dorm parents.

The journey began with getting my suitcase packed. In my early years my mother packed my suitcase. This is where I received a **second blessing** as an MK, and that was learning how to get the most stuff in a suitcase as only my mother knew how!

Before leaving, of course I said good-by to our pet monkey. When I walked the cute little baby monkey hung on tightly to my leg. He was my baby doll! The little darling loved to be held and cuddled in all my doll blankets. As a little girl I would feed him mashed bananas with a doll spoon and dress him in doll clothes. This was my **third blessing** as an MK! Who today, as a child, gets to have something like a real live doll that is all cuddly and loving and adorable?

But the dread of the final day settled in as we drove the long two miles down the dusty road to arrive at the dirt-covered runway, which had a wood shelter with corrugated metal for an airport terminal. My heart would feel like lead and inside I would be breaking apart. (When I was six I traveled with my older brother, but later it was with my younger brother also.)

I can still see my mother with sunglasses and a white hanky, which she would use to wave "good-bye" as we boarded the airplane. I never knew until later that the sunglasses were for her to hide her tears. She wanted us to not suffer by seeing her cry.

We would hug and kiss and then climb up into the two-engine Laotian commercial plane and fly to Vientiane, the capital of Laos, sometimes for an overnight stay, but most often we'd leave from Vientiane just as soon as we arrived.

Regarding the Sayaboury airport where we lived, there was no airport tower and only a dirt runway. Often we had to wait for a water buffalo, or elephants or people to get off the dirt runway. People used the runway to pass through to their villages.

Most of the time the Laotians traveling with us had live caged chickens and bags of merchandise all over airplane aisle. As a small child of six, it was quite a hardship to climb over the piles of merchandise packing the aisle. I remember some of the merchandise was hundreds of cheap plastic dolls packed in cloth bags.

I was terrified of flying since the area we traveled in had very, very thick fog and sheer mountains on both sides. In my little girl's mind I imagined what it would be like to crash on the sides of those giant mountains. The pilots relied only on their instrument panel in the cockpit. There were no radio towers anywhere to guide the airplane.

Amazingly out of all those 12 airplane rides per year from six years old until I was 14 there was never a near disaster! God was always protecting us! I learned a promise in the Bible in Psalm 102:28a, "The children of your servants shall dwell secure."

After leaving my parents I cried for a while, but even as a six year old, I knew and trusted that this plan was from God and I knew my job was to believe and trust God to keep us safe even though I was terrified.

The entire trip usually took two or three days. My brothers and I stayed in two guesthouses—one in Vientiane, Laos (especially if my dad accompanied us), and the other in Saigon, Vietnam. In Vientiane, six more MKs joined my brothers and me. When this happened, we often flew immediately to Saigon. This trip was repeated four times a year, with a total of twelve airplane rides back and forth to school for two semesters.

I remember vividly the deep cut in my heart by the time we reached Saigon. The heat in Saigon was unbearable with temperatures in the nineties with 100% humidity. The terrible humidity and high heat made it impossible to sleep. Sleeping on sheets in such heat and humidity made one feel very sweaty! Many times it was more comfortable to sleep under the ceiling fan on the cold tile floors with a pillow for my head. There I'd fall asleep heartbroken and afraid of what would happen during the next five months!

From Saigon we flew in a bigger four-engine Vietnamese plane. Back then one couldn't see very well in the airplane or breathe because of the sickening fog and smell of cigarette-smoking passengers. Thinking of it now makes me feel sick to my stomach.

On one occasion we were flying with a group of MKs from Saigon to our school in the mountains of Vietnam where our boarding school was located, in the tourist city of Dalat, and somehow I was the last to board the airplane. There were no seats left! I was already crying in my heart. No one gave up his or her seat to a tiny eight-year-old girl! Instead, a rather large Frenchman indicated for me to sit on his knee. I had no other choice, and totally embarrassed, I sat there the entire two-hour flight to Dalat. One might wonder why God would allow this, or why no one tried to help me—but I survived that interesting trip sitting on that man's knee.

The man never said a word the entire trip and I remember clearly he kept his hands totally away from me. I do remember it was the most uncomfortable plane ride I have ever had. But at least I was not left behind, and for all I know, maybe the man was actually an angel sent to give me a place to sit. The Bible tells us that God's thoughts are not our thoughts neither are His ways our ways (Isaiah 55:8).

Actually this has made for an interesting story for me to tell to friends, which comes to my **fourth blessing** in being an MK—adventure! Life in America becomes so predictable—boring, one could call it. Life as an MK was always an adventure, not only in experiencing the unexpected, but also in learning about all kinds of different cultures. Although going through so much trial and inner pain, I can now say that God meant it all for my good.

Oh, beautiful, elegant Dalat! Though filled with grief and loneliness, I will never ever forget seeing and experiencing the awesome privilege of living in Dalat, among absolutely gorgeous French villas owned as vacation homes by French millionaires! My favorite memory is of driving down the main French boulevard and seeing each gorgeous mansion covered with the brilliant bougainvillea and the elegant French architecture.

From the early 1900s until the late 1950s, most of South East Asia was a colony of France. Consequently French was the second language. With the French influence much of the architecture all over Dalat was very elegant. The most outstanding building was the French hotel, which overlooked the Dalat Lake. From the hotel's beautiful chandeliers inside and the elegant French style exterior, this hotel was gorgeous. The French hotel looked like a castle.

Taking the two mile drive down the Boulevard, lined with gorgeous French villas with lovely yards full of rose bushes, our large van would take the right turn and in about a minute one saw off on the hill the beautiful original French mansion that was boarding school—my new home.

The Dalat School dining hall was downstairs and our teachers lived upstairs. The other buildings were dormitory-style stucco buildings nestled among tall pines. It was a beautiful place with stone walls and French doors. I loved it instantly! This is the **fifth blessing** for me, to be privileged to live among these beautiful buildings, gardens full of flowers, and rose arbors.

My favorite memory was listening to the wind as it whistled through those tall pines, which tempered the hot weather and humidity of the lowlands of Saigon. The average temperature was always around 70° Fahrenheit, although during the rainy season it got just a slight bit cooler.

I remember Dalat with pleasure. I have always been interested in adventure and awed by majesty, such as was found in the gorgeous French mansions and the mysterious sound of the whistling wind! This is my **blessing number six**—the privilege of imagination and pretending that allowed me to think I was really a princess and rich (although I only owned about three dresses). It was a blessing because it helped to ease my pain by living among the beauty of the pine covered hills and the beautiful villas.

Another exciting feeling for me about being in Dalat was that I was actually born there on October 28, 1950, in the lovely French hospital by Dalat Lake after my parents, along with hundreds of other missionaries, were forced to leave China.

The Vietnamese doctor who delivered me was the King's doctor of Viet Nam. The Dalat School nurse, Miss Chandler, assisted at the doctor's side, helping deliver me into this wonderful world of beauty and adventure.

So Dalat was special to me! But I knew I was now facing about five months without my dear mother and father. The first two weeks I cried myself to sleep every single night.

Chapter 2
Rules, Ridicule and Rejection

Amazingly in about three weeks, I forgot about missing my parents—that is until the verbal abuse and bullying started coming from my roommates or others. Today I know that those who bullied, whether consciously or unconsciously, were hurting also because of the lack of their fathers and mothers. But back then, all I remember is that a couple of kids consistently taunted, laughed at me, and told me that I was ugly. I forgive them now. They are among my best friends and I pray for them every day. But for months all I wanted to do was run away!

In the girl's dorm we had assigned chores for cleaning the room we shared with two to four girls. We had bunk beds in some rooms and iron single beds in other rooms.

One night, just after going to bed in the first grade girl's boarding school room (which was located just across the hall from the school nurse), I did something that tells me a lot about myself.

I enjoyed being active, and because of that, did not want to go to bed.

I remember getting out of bed after the lights went out to play with my dolls. After about ten minutes I stepped out into the hallway. Suddenly there stood the school nurse!

She asked me what was I doing being up after the lights were out. I answered with a half-lie. I said, "I was over there," pointing to my bedroom. I was ashamed but the nurse was very kind and patiently led me back to my bedroom where I promptly fell asleep and never did that again.

The dorm parents made life fun by motivating the girls from each room to keep their room clean by making a game of it. The game comprised of a pretty house or little girl outlined on heavy poster board and then hung by a hook on each dorm room door. If our jobs were done well for the week our room would receive in the outline of a house on our door one of the following: a sofa, a bed, a lamp, a rug, pictures on the walls, etc. and for the little girl she would receive a pretty curls, a hat, a sweater, a coat, gloves, socks and shoes, etc. Every semester was a different game for example getting things while on a hike in the woods and many other inventive games.

Our daily jobs were sweeping, dusting, making our beds tidy, and keeping all dresser tops in order. Also the things in our drawers had to be kept tidy every day.

One rule was that we had to make our beds with hospital corners. A few times our drawers or beds were not made right, so when we returned from class all the clothes from the drawers would be dumped on the floor and our bedding torn off the beds. It didn't bother me much at the time, but I remember my roommates complaining a lot.

I don't know why, but in my class of six girls, we never once won for having the cleanest room. I know I was always very particular about being neat but if everyone else was doing it a different way, I always followed and didn't do my chores as I was ordered.

This rule of getting marks against you for a messy room continued all the way up to grade nine. I remember adults telling us that those who had graduated before us were perfect housekeepers. I believe this training worked for our good because I have been in many MK homes in later years and have seen that they are lovely and elegant.

I thank God every day for the finest examples of the Christian life that most of the dorm parents exhibited while I was at Dalat. I never heard arguments between the dorm parents. They cheered us with smiles and a friendly "Hello" throughout each day. **Blessing number seven** is witnessing the finest examples of selfless Christ-likeness in the teachers, dorm parents, and staff of Dalat School.

I remember in the first grade I developed a very badly decayed tooth, which unfortunately could only be taken out by someone taking me on a quick trip to the dentist in Saigon. I remember feeling so much uncertainty about going all by myself as a six year old. But to be with Uncle Archie Mitchell (the head dorm parent) was the nicest, kindest person you would ever want! I didn't feel lonely or sad when I was with him!

I have never forgotten Uncle Archie's kindness in buying me a Vietnamese doll and a book about Noah that included a record that played the story. (Remember those old record players with a needle, which brought out the music or words?) He bought these pretty gifts just to show how much he cared for me and was sad to see me have to endure the painful time at the dentist. How blessed I was! How kind my dorm parents were!

This brings me to **blessing number eight**— the many kindnesses of my dorm parents who had such a wonderful influence on my life, even to this day. I wanted to grow up to be just like my dorm parents! What a blessing they were! How they worked so hard to take away our loneliness by planning exciting Friday night events!

I remember a time around the third grade (at that time I roomed with different roommates—not the ones who bullied me), when I was obsessed with ballet after watching Carol Heiss, who starred in the Disney movie, *Snow White and the Three Stooges.* This obsession took entire afternoons and evenings of my time. I obtained an encyclopedia, which showed the different ballet steps. Then with Stravinsky played on the record player, my roommates would invite the dorm mother and other girls to come to watch our choreographed ballet. I was living in the world of being a real live ballerina.

Oh, how I loved to pretend I was a gorgeous ballerina dancing to classical music! This brings me to **blessing number nine,** which is the blessing of seeing beauty, even if only in my imagination.

Often Sunday afternoons, after 4:00, a friend and I would go down to the empty auditorium and pretend we were beautiful soloists and sing to the empty chairs. My favorite solo was "One Day."

My obsession with beauty and gracefulness caused me to enjoy swinging my hips to feel my skirt as it brushed the back of my legs. It's really true! I swung my hips back and forth as I walked. It made me feel beautiful until a guy up in the high school grades told me not to do it. It must have looked silly and I was glad he said something. I remember that I immediately stopped.

Something I didn't know until I became an adult is that God often uses imagination (where one can pretend they live in a different world) as a healer of some of our deepest wounds. However, living in a pretend world as an escape from pain is not a very happy life.

I saw that real joy came not by escaping from my pain by pretending, but by learning of the deep wounds in other MKs hearts, and encouraging them to trust God. He loved them! He would help them with their problems through prayer. I saw that God had allowed my trials, to learn to forgive and to trust God to go on in life by turning my attention to other MKs who were hurting as I was. He was helping me to get out of self-pity and to be involved with others. I say this now—that all along God was strengthening me during the trials I endured.

However, not all my experiences with my dorm parents held good memories. We were warned that if our rooms were not cleaned by the next day of room-check, we would all get a spanking. The worst day of my life was when I came up to my room during class to get my homework, which I had forgotten. While I was getting my homework the dorm parent decided to spank me then and there for the messy room. About ten minutes later I returned to the classroom and received two public spankings for presenting late homework in two subjects. The spanking by the teacher was applied by bending down and holding my ankles and then the teacher gave me a whack or two on the behind. Inside my heart I couldn't bear the isolation and humiliation I felt that day. I hid my pain all day. No one knew, but after school, I cried and cried and cried.

Later on I found out that the dorm parent completely forgot about my other roommates deserving spankings for not having a clean dorm room. I could never figure out all this because I always tried to keep my part of the room neat. If several didn't do their duty, then we all received the spanking. On this particular day there was no justice. That sorrowful day taught me that sometimes in life there might not be any justice.

After the light went out there was a rule about not talking or playing. Many nights we were spanked on our bare behinds with a ruler or a hairbrush. I remember some of my roommates after the spanking saying that they were laughing in their pillows. But I was always very ashamed of getting spanked.

Have you ever jumped off the top of a wardrobe closet onto a spring mattress? I remember the wardrobe was about six feet tall. My one roommate, who was so mean, was jumping off the closet on to the bed when suddenly the dorm parent was there. I remember a spanking was given to us even though not all of us had jumped off the cupboard onto the bed. But this particular roommate always thought the spankings were funny.

On another occasion, the head of Dalat School grabbed me off the seesaw in full view of every one who was also playing there. I was the age of seven and was standing there in the middle of the seesaw. I didn't know what I had done wrong. The dorm parent paddled me right in front of everyone. The head dorm parent scolded me loudly saying that it was against the rules. I felt so ashamed. I had disobeyed. If only someone had told me, I would not have stood anywhere on the seesaw!

I wasn't the only one who got in trouble. People walked along the road, which followed next to the fence at the bottom of our school property, and once a stone fight began between a Dalat

School boy and the Vietnamese kids on the road. I was there and saw it all. Unfortunately, "Be sure your sins will find you out," because he got bloodied badly by a stone, and thus the truth came out and he was disciplined.

Disobeying the rule of going off school property without permission and without being accompanied by an adult has caused irreparable damage to some. I came close to a dangerous situation myself, although it was by being naive. Because of my vivid imagination from reading too many Nancy Drew books, I crawled under the fence into the massive flowerbeds of the enormous mansion next to our school property. My adventure was to play detective all by myself. How exciting it was for me to crawl on my belly and imagine that there was a light that would go off and on up in the attic of the five story mansion. What were they doing? Perhaps it was a secret place where they counterfeited money? Or maybe they had kidnapped someone and kept the person in the attic. On a few occasions I brought a friend with me. We crawled all around on our bellies whispering about crimes being done and how we were going to catch them and take them to the police!

This would be an amusing story but for the fact that it was very, very dangerous and stupid for me and my friend to do this! God was protecting us and kept us safe. There were others who went off the Dalat school property unattended and the consequences were very, very sad indeed!

Unfair discipline and doing dumb things are real experiences for MKs who are without the protection and attention of their parents. Who was there to go and talk to when we had to deal with the consequences? Sometimes all a child needs is to unload his heartache to a good listener and after that he feels like his heartache is gone, because there is someone who understands. Mothers and fathers know their children inside and out and are better equipped to truly understand the situation.

One night all my roommates were rather noisy. In fact, I think this was the time the dorm parent walked in just as one of my roommates was swinging on the door by holding onto the handle after lights were out and we were supposed to be in bed sleeping! We will never forget the anger of the dorm parent because she immediately marched in and moved all our beds (they were iron beds with wheels) from one end of the room to the other. Now all of our beds were in one corner. Some of my roommates thought it hilarious, but I was very ashamed.

Bells! Bells! Bells! Bells to wake up; bells to go to breakfast; bells for school to begin; bells for recess; bells for lunch; bells for afternoon school; bells for evening supper; and then bells to go to bed. I think these loud military-style screaming bells frightened me most when I first arrived as a little six-year-old girl.

There was one rule that was nonnegotiable and that rule was that each child from six years old and up, had to write home every week on Sunday afternoon.

It was a pain for me because every week everything was boring or there were things I wanted to say but I was afraid of retribution. I remember telling my parents in every letter how much fun it was to play on the monkey bars, and then I filled up the entire letter with Os and Xs (hugs and kisses). No one ever said anything, but to this day writing letters is not my most favorite thing to do.

Sunday afternoons were a day of rest so we had to just sit on our beds and do nothing until 4:00. One day in grade three, I couldn't stand the boredom any longer. I dressed myself like a bride and pretended I was getting married. Oh, it was so much fun to pretend, but reality stepped in, when in walked the dorm parent. Remember, we were supposed to sit or lie down and not do anything. I was so petrified I dove under the bed. I don't remember getting a spanking, but I did receive a very long lecture about staying still.

One extraordinary thing my roommates credited me for was the ability to put them to sleep by making up stories. As I mentioned earlier, I have an incredible imagination. Just several years ago an MK told me that she always enjoyed the stories I told while the lights were out as my roommates each slowly dropped off to sleep. I saw that God had given me a gift of story telling. This is **blessing number ten.**

My greatest pain came from the two roommates who would taunt me, mimic me with a funny voice, and laugh at me, saying what I was saying was dumb. What was the blessing in this?

Before I continue with my story, I want to say some things in defense of those who criticize, put-down, and reject their peers. My roommates were in fact hurting also, perhaps angered over a favored sibling, or from the feelings of vulnerability one feels without mother or father. The feelings of vulnerability might have made them feel the need to gain power over others. I don't know what it was, but I was filled with anguish and a deep sense of insecurity and began to withdraw and become introverted.

It has been suggested to me by other MKs that

they had observed that those with dominating, extroverted personalities had a happier life as an MK; whereas the shy, introverted, artistic personality (such as myself) were greatly bullied— and some never recovered from their experiences at Dalat School.

But the greatest factor I believe in a successful Dalat School student was having parents hundreds of miles away who themselves were walking in faith with God, praying daily for their children. Now it is true that parents are sinful just like their children, because the Bible says in Romans 3:23, "For all have sinned and fall short of the glory of God." But the children of parents who truly trusted God and didn't worry, later on in life continued to walk with God, never rebelling against God or their parents.

There is nothing worse for children than parents who put on a show of godliness by praying long prayers in prayer meetings, then quarrel and gossip all the time but never make it right with God or those they hurt through gossip! Gossip, though it may be true is still sin. It is listed in 2 Corinthians 12:20, "For I fear...that perhaps there may be quarreling, anger, hostility, slander, gossip, conceit and disorder." Regarding "gossip," would you like all your "dirty laundry" spread all over the neighborhood? 1 John 4:20a states, "If anyone says 'I love God' and hates his brother, he is a liar;" and also 1 John 3:6b, "No one who keeps on sinning has either seen him or known him." Christians who keep on sinning in these ways are acting like hypocrites. It is seen as just a religion. The children just see people putting up a front to impress others with their spirituality.

Also regarding the dorm parents, they were not at fault in the least for my problems. How could they possibly watch all 60 girls, ages 6-18, 100% of the time after school or before bedtime? The years I attended Dalat School and experienced these things were from 1956 to 1969. In the 1980s, I believe Dalat School began to add additional staff to watch over groups of about 12 students each. I think this ratio did wonders for the lives and the futures of later Dalat School students.

One time one of the girls, just to have a good time, teased me mercilessly by hitting me with a jump rope, laughing at me and watching to see what I would do. I remember trying to grab the jump rope, but I stumbled and the laughter grew louder. I was mocked on a daily base. At the time I couldn't understand why.

Whenever I followed my roommates, they would stop, turn around and give me a stony stare. If I kept following them to play with them they would continue to stop and give me this stony stare. The statement was obvious—*we don't want you hanging around us.* Oh, how my heart would break! I liked them and wanted to be with them! But God has His reasons for allowing such rejection, and I often would pray to God to teach me to learn how to deal with my aching heart and forgive them.

For one thing I was very quiet, and very plain looking. I remember one day I had the flu, and while alone in the room, I put a mirror up close to my face and decided I was the ugliest girl! Besides this, I was often called "ugly" and "stupid." Because of my shortness, I appeared chubby. There was no feeling of personal self-worth, so I never showered and I think I only washed my hair twice one semester.

The questions arise, *how could all this really happen? And is the blame on myself?* Yes, this is true; but when one becomes so depressed and there are no parents there to love and encourage one tenderly, one becomes neurotic and fears further retribution from one's peers.

One afternoon I heard some girls quietly whispering in a bathroom stall. There was a bathtub in the stall, and they stayed in there a long time doing something. To find out I was too afraid. I knew in my heart something definitely was not right. Experiences such as this could be why I never took a bath or washed my hair.

During this time often bathrooms were lacking running water and also there were not enough bathtubs. Everyone got there before me. No one gave me personal attention because after all, how could one adult couple take individual care of sixty girls from ages 6-18? Impossible!

So I had body odor, and besides that, in the upper elementary grades I began growing two teeth above my eyeteeth in the front of my mouth. You know what I was called then? "Fangs!" I cannot describe to you the complete loneliness I felt. No one wanted me and I felt like running away. There was absolutely no motivation to improve myself because no one cared. I was indeed in great grief of heart for months.

One day I went to an adult for counseling. She said, "Don't you think this is something you need to trust God with?" Now of course this is true, but I perceived an impersonal pat answer and negative attitude behind the words. I don't remember any empathy, sincere sorrow, or loving kindness. There is no substitute for a real mother and father. Another adult may try their best but they will never love a child as a parent loves their own child!

This lack of a parental figure cannot be more seen or needed as when I describe one of my loneliest times at Dalat. Suddenly it started— every night in the middle of the night when the whole dorm was silent and still, I would wake up with an intense need to vomit!

I was so afraid of causing anyone problems that with all my effort and strong discipline, I made myself run to the bathroom, three rooms down the hall. I will never forget to this day how I struggled to keep the vomit from coming, and in the process couldn't run straight and ended up crashing from one side of the hall to the other in order to get to the bathroom. Before it came out, I always made it! But that was just the beginning of torture as I stood there after vomiting every-thing up, with dry heaves that went on for about half an hour. Oh, how I needed the love and comfort of my own mother and father!

Because I was so terribly sick, I knocked on an adult's door to get a pill or a cracker to help my stomach. The response was, "Well, you'll be all right now, just go back to bed." Unfortunately this same experience went on for at least a month.

After weeks of this torture someone decided I had an ulcer and began a special diet, but the nightly torture continued. Finally, a smart thinking person thought of a condition very prevalent in Vietnam, which was worms. Sure enough, after a month of nightly torture I received a full dose of worm medicine and the awful suffering completely stopped.

This kind of trial was hard but to my mind it was much easier to take than the constant bullying I received from my classmates. I know they were hurting too, so I forgave them and just went and found someone else with greater needs than myself. This brings me to **blessing number eleven.** The best way I have to describe this blessing is to quote a poem:

Whom God Chooses
by Henry F. Lyte (1793-1847)

When God wants to drill a man,
and thrill a man, and skill a man,
When God wants to mold a man,
To play the noblest part;
When He yearns with all His heart
To create so great and bold a man,
That all the world shall be amazed,
Watch His methods; watch His ways.

How He ruthlessly perfects
When He royally elects!
How He hammers him and hurts him

And with mighty blows converts him
Into trial shapes of clay
Which only God understands;
While his tortured heart is crying,
And he lifts beseeching hands!

How He bends but never breaks
When His good He undertakes.
How He uses whom He chooses,
And with every purpose fuses him;
But every act induces him
To try His splendor out—
God knows what He's about!
Go then, earthly fame and treasure!

Come disaster, scorn, and pain!
In Thy service, pain is pleasure;
With Thy favor, loss is gain.
I have called Thee, Abba, Father;
I have stayed my heart on Thee.
Storms may howl, and clouds may gather;
All must work for good to me.

"God chooses and abuses who He wants to mold into a real diamond to reflect His glory." Trials can be for our good if we allow ourselves to get better by them and not become bitter by them. In fact, Romans 5:3-4 says, "Suffering produces endurance and endurance produces character and character produces hope and hope does not put us to shame, because God's love has been poured into our hearts through the Holy Spirit who has been given to us."

Blessing number twelve came when I trusted Jesus to save me from my sins at the age of eight. However, my life never was totally changed to the extent that I spent daily time in God's Word on my own. My spiritual life was an up-and-down experience until later, when at the beginning of my sophomore year at Toccoa Falls Bible College I totally committed my life to Jesus. From that time I never turned back from following Jesus Christ with all my heart!

But while I attended Dalat, I tried to see what God was saying to me in my struggles. One thought was maybe I must learn something that I could use to help another who was hurting. I knew the verse in Corinthians 1:3-4 which says, "Blessed be the God and Father of our Lord Jesus Christ, the God of mercies and God of all comfort, who comforts us in all our afflictions, so that we may be able to comfort those who are in affliction, with the comfort with which we ourselves are comforted by God." I knew that God would use the lessons I was learning from being bullied to encourage others. **Blessing number thirteen** was, knowing for myself that God was teaching me lessons through my trials to forgive and love, as Jesus Christ would want me to love!

The big "SELF" was pretty big in me. God wanted me to learn submission to what He was doing in my life—submission to forgive, submission without a word to any verbal abuse—in other words being meek. This modern day thinking teaches that meekness means to be weak. However, the Bible teaches in Luke 6:32-33, "If you love those who love you, what benefit is that to you? For even sinners love those who love them. If you do good to those who do good to you, what benefit is that to you? For even sinners do the same." In other words, it shows more strength in a person who controls his tongue and forgives without a word than the one who is showing power by putting down others.

Anyone can allow tempers to flare and engage in a fistfight. What does it actually accomplish except more hatred? Someone has to make the first move to stop the hate, and that is so hard to do unless Jesus Christ abides in us to change our natural reaction. Our natural reaction will always be to retort with words or actually resort to a real fistfight.

When we are unjustly treated we must accept the pain, forgive the ones who hurt us, and let them go free. If thoughts of revenge are allowed to continue without the willingness to choose to forgive the one who does the bullying, the problem could actually escalate to our doing regrettable actions which may effect us for the rest of our lives—maybe even resulting in prison.

I'm so grateful for how God taught me through all my hardship that the only recourse was to be silent and in my heart to forgive. God did this for me in truth because later, when I was several years older, I was able to become best friends with the two who gave me such trials.

I am blessed today with a heart of love for all my MK classmates. Actually in truth, I was the one who was so blessed by the things they taught me and motivated me kindly in the areas of hygiene. I remember crying out to God to please help me look better, because of my double teeth, acne, dirty hair, etc.

This comes to the **fourteenth blessing,** which was when God answered a prayer that meant so much to me personally. "Fangs!" I was teased so much for double teeth growing straight out on top of teeth beneath. Oh, how much I prayed that a dentist could do something for my teeth. But it was impossible because missionaries live on a very low salary.

You can guess God's miracle for me! One day I was at the dentist in Bangkok with my parents, and I don't think my parents even had to ask about the double teeth, because the dentist quickly presented a simple plan to keep the eyeteeth, which were the "Fangs." The dentist said the eyeteeth were the most important teeth in the mouth. The good dentist removed the teeth underneath and saved the eyeteeth! God made the former "fangs" to grow down perfectly into the place to where the previous teeth were removed (although it took a while)! Soon my front teeth were perfectly aligned. What a gracious and loving God I had! I could smile now because I wanted also other people to be happy.

One thing I hated more than anything was my last name, which was "Tubbs." One time a girl made fun of me by saying she wanted to blow her nose in a bath Tubbs. Many others called me "Tubby."

The mocking, bullying, and teasing got to be so bad that I never stayed in my room after classes were over, but played outside the whole afternoon. This is where I have my best memories. I really had a ton of fun playing cowboys and Indians with the boys and a few girls.

Because we lived among pine trees, the roots made wonderful places to cover with branches to make cool forts. Pine cones were the bullets and if you were hit you played dead. We also captured the other side, persons who became prisoners. This is where I spent most of my time to avoid ridicule.

I remember always praying for God to stop the ridicule and help me. The verse that encouraged me during this time was Matthew 19:30, "But many who are first will be last, and the last first."

I began to look for other girls who were outcasts as I was. This brings me to **blessing number fifteen.** God was teaching me to love the hurting. Ever since this time in my life, my blessing in life has been to cheer for the "underdog." I think now that it is a wonderful blessing that I was hated and went through so much ridicule because now I know how others feel when they go through that, too.

I learned I could empathize especially with the dear lonely people in our nation's nursing homes and other people who are hated, if for no reason than they are of a different color or facial features which do not match the fashion of the day! These are all blessings—to love the unloved, to cheer the downcast, to take notice of those who need encouragement, and to do something as simple as to write a short encouraging note.

Because of all the abuse I took, God has given me the gift of mercy. There was a time I knew what it was like to want mercy. I understand those who are shut out of society because they were different. So during those lonely years, like Jacob of old who thought every thing was against him, God was really working out a plan that would bring back blessings a hundredfold—more than I could have ever imagined!

Chapter 3
Life in the Classroom, Dining Hall and Weekends

Humiliation is the only word to describe it! The teacher brought my desk away from everyone else's desk and put it right next to hers.

I felt like I was isolated and singled out as dumb. The reason? I was so terrible in math that my teacher put me in front of the class to condescendingly (I felt) work with me on my math while she taught everyone else in class.

School was pleasant most of the time except for when it came to math and the sciences. I was always very good but I had a lot of trouble staying focused. No mother or father present meant that I was my own motivator, which meant that often my homework was unfinished. It wasn't that I was trying to be bad. I just was so depressed that just the thought of homework was enough to make me almost quit life.

One day in science class I was unable to verbalize to the teacher the difference between the rotation of the earth and the revolution of the earth around the sun. Perhaps I did not know—or maybe I was too petrified to answer in class—or I got my wording wrong. The teacher told me to get up and pretend the desk was the sun and turn myself around and around in a rotation while, moving also around my desk in a revolution. I have never forgotten the complete humiliation I felt. These were during the years I had double teeth, a bad complexion, and dirty hair. As I rotated around the desk I heard snickering coming from all over the classroom.

The other area I had a problem with in math was in problem solving. What made it worse was I always gave the wrong answer and then everyone would giggle and smirk. I concluded that if any person was smart in math, they must be considered brilliant by everyone.

Now I know God made everyone with strengths and weaknesses. But at that time people called me "stupid," and would circle their finger by their ear, implying I was dimwitted.

I coped by being an excellent reader. Reading also became an escape from the wounded heart I felt in school. This brings me to **blessing number sixteen.** Being a good reader has helped me in every way as I learned from the stories of other people who grew up in worse situations than mine.

Reading is still my favorite pastime as I have a one hundred volume library of antique classics and old stories from around the early 1900s. In these old stories are many good examples of how people endured hardship. Authors Charles Dickens, Federol Dostoevsky, Jane Austin, and Leon Tolstoy are some examples.

Another interesting pastime as a child was collecting tadpoles and putting them in a shallow cookie tin. Though no one else cared, I had my tiny tadpole friends. When they began to grow little feet I would carefully deliver them outside to a natural pond.

One of my saddest days came when, as an eight year old, I came into my room as I always did to visit my tadpoles, and to my dismay and utter sadness I discovered that one of my tadpole's tails was smashed!

To the credit of Dalat School, they focused on heart issues of all MKs by having revival services every semester. Following one revival during a semester a roommate who had bullied me told me she had crushed my tadpole's tail because she was jealous of me.

I don't fault the teachers for my frustrations in school as they were serving God by teaching the children of missionaries, always with a salary much less than if they had the same job in the

US. They did their very best to educate us and they loved us!

I know the dorm parents carried immense burdens as they felt the great responsibility of parenting and mentoring so many children. It must have been an awesome job for my teachers and dorm parents.

Our teachers had a good idea to brighten our school days. In the dining hall were large wood trays filled to the brim with sliced French bread, spread with homemade peanut butter and then topped with cinnamon and sugar. M-m-m-m! This was a delightful treat during our ten-minute recess and was so healthy. I can remember this treat was always there, every day of the week at recess time. Someone cared enough to spend time every day, slicing and fixing these delicious treats to brighten our school days. How wonderful and good God was to all of us MKs!

A favorite dorm parent was Uncle Gene Evans. He was a comedian to match any of the funniest on TV. In fact he looked and acted somewhat like Dick Van Dyke. I think it was his wonderful sense of humor that got many of us MKs through the four to five month semesters.

Every weekend the adults worked hard at creating Friday Night Fun Night. The dorm room talent show they let us put on was one of my favorite memories. I remember the clothes modeling show our room put on when I was in the fifth grade. Uncle Gene made it hilarious by changing our names as we modeled. I felt like a celebrity when he would introduce us with a classy sounding name! When I modeled my modest, one-piece bathing suit and came sashaying out, he introduced me as Miss Vantubbsenhagen. I decided I wished I could really have that name, and to my surprise my wish actually almost came true. My one and only dear husband's last name is Van Valkenburg. I'll bet Uncle Gene never thought he'd come so close to being a prophet!

Another fun night was Halloween. Next to Dalat School were tunnels carved out by the Japanese. One of our Halloween events was getting to go through a tunnel with ghoulish sounds made by the high school guys, and also with fake spiders, wet spaghetti, fake bats, spider webs, and skeletons.

The teachers and dorm parents often put together wonderful festive fairs! There must have been 10-15 booths with games like toss the ring, throw the ball into the net, bob for apples, or a booth with a story teller. Some adults put on special performances. Miss Kelck memorized and then professionally dramatized a story. Uncle Gene sang in a great barbershop quartet. Oh, what fun!

I can see two blessings in the next two stories. Our school was blessed with a dear couple who were the directors of the school for many years. They were the Fitzstevens. Auntie Esther, as we called her (anyone who was an adult we called Auntie or Uncle), learned French cooking as an MK growing up in Hanoi, North Vietnam. I count her as **blessing number seventeen.**

She was tall and slender with red hair, and was as beautiful as an angel. I loved her because she loved us. As I grew older, she was the one I wanted to grow up to be exactly like!

And our sweet and kind cook, Mr. Bep, is **blessing number eighteen.** Auntie Esther was able to teach our wonderful Vietnamese cook Mr. Bep how to make chocolate éclairs, delicious roast beef with scrumptious mashed potatoes, French pies, lemon meringue desserts, and also my favorite Vietnamese "Chaios" and "Soup Shing Wha."

Mr. Bep also learned how to make wonderful ice cream when someone shipped a commercial size ice cream maker to the school.

On Sunday evenings we always had the most tasty pancakes, followed by the well-known "Dalat School Special," which was sliced bananas in milk sweetened with sweetened condensed milk.

Sometimes Mr. Bep would let us come in and watch him cook and sometimes we received a treat of a spoon full of sugar. He was always faithful and loved God, along with all his family. He was God's blessing to all of us MKs.

But meals were not always pleasant because, since I was a very slow eater, I was usually the last person to finish eating in the dining room. This was a miserable time for me, feeling so lonely and isolated.

The main problem was that we had to finish all the food on our plates. Since pineapple was cheap, it was served almost every day for dessert or on a lettuce leaf or mixed with fruit. I never acquired a taste for Vietnamese pineapple. It was not sweet and it made my tongue prickle like I was eating needles.

Everyone got to sleep in Saturday morning. But my fondest memory is of the large serving bowl heaped up with glutinous rice (sticky rice) for Saturday breakfast. On this rice we could drizzle on as much sweetened condensed milk as we wanted, and on the very top we spooned chopped peanuts. The taste was something between "Pay Day" chocolate bars and French nougats. M-m-m . . . so delicious!

Regarding our diet however, I remember my

roommates complaining about how it was full of carbohydrates. I agreed with them. I also hated the milk because our milk was made out of powdered milk, and in order to save money, there was hardly any powdered milk in the water! It was like cloudy water and it tasted like rubber smells.

In fact, this diet could be the reason why every time I went to Dalat School, I never ovulated once. But when I returned home to my parents where I received love and good food, I would always ovulate! It was years later that I learned that a tumor was growing next to my pituitary. This kind of tumor, I learned, can be caused by extreme stress. Due to this tumor, I suffered in later years by not being able to have children. I finally ovulated when I took Bromocryptine, which is prescribed to shrink this kind of tumor. After taking this drug, I became pregnant with our only son. Being sent away hundreds of miles from one's parents often make the children of missionaries pay a very high price! To this day I am so thankful that God gave my husband and me at least one child—a wonderful son named Samuel John, which means, "asked of God" and "gift of God!"

Death came very close to me at Dalat School when I was eight years old. I must have been nearly unconscious because I don't remember how I got to the clinic's special sick room. All I remember is not being able to see clearly and feeling as though I was in a dream. My fever was 104° going on 105°. The two nurses worked on me the entire night, cooling my body with cold towels which were dipped in a bathtub filled with melting icecubes. I never noticed the cold. My mind was swirling and I knew nothing. How those two nurses must have prayed while they worked, because by morning my fever began to break. In times like this a child surely needs their mother and father. But I am truly thankful for the love and faithfulness shown to me by those two nurses. They stayed up the entire night to take care of me. I am so very grateful for them!

There were many things that helped so much in dealing with the heartache of being told I was ugly and dumb! One of these things was the wonderful roller skating area located just outside the classrooms. The joy of skating fast made me forget all my troubles. The adults even planned roller skating parties where music was broadcast through a public address system. It was a delicious feeling to know how to skate faster and better than anyone else!

I'll never forget the old fashioned Friday night

taffy pulls. Can you picture about sixty kids running around outside with warm taffy, pulling it until it was just the right color and ready to eat? My mouth is watering just thinking of it!

There were also the hikes to "The Three Hills" or "Jackson Mountain" for a marshmallow roast where we also enjoyed hotdogs and then played "Capture the Flag" and "Kick the Can" until after dark. Sure, there were tigers out in the woods and King Cobra snakes—but we never gave them a second thought.

We also enjoyed so many planned events, like outdoor barbecues by the grill pit, all-day bike rides around Dalat Lake, and drives to Prenn Falls which had a walking path behind the falls. There was also a great zoo next to Prenn Falls. The school even took us once on an all-day trip to the beach where there was unending sand stretching for miles and not a soul in sight! We all got overly sunburned because someone forgot the suntan lotion. I remember my roommate had terrible blisters all over her shoulder, arms, and face. I felt so sorry for her. But we would never have given up that trip to the ocean. These planned events are all **blessing number nineteen.**

We had two rather terrifying events for the girls. Our school owned a chimpanzee that was vicious and would bite. One day he got loose and somehow or other made his way down into the girls dorm hall. You never heard such door banging and screams in your life! I was terrified too! Dalat School also had a mean horse named "Dolly." You couldn't get near her or else she would bite you. One time she got loose and tore up and down the school property at a fierce gallop. We all had to run—otherwise she would knock us down and/or bite. No one could catch her!

However, whenever we were terribly bored, we'd take a walk down to see Dolly, but just to look. And, as a side note, on the way to see Dolly, we would pass by the back of the kitchen where we visited all the nice Vietnamese women who helped cook and do our laundry. We liked them because of their friendly smiles and we enjoyed trying our limited Vietnamese on them.

In conclusion, as MKs, we will never know the amount of sacrifice all of the dorm parents gave just to help us get a good night's rest and/or to give us a night of fun we would never forget. I know I haven't forgotten!

In all my trials there is one very special person I could never have done without and that special person is my younger brother Paul. He is twenty-one months younger than myself. He, I know, struggled with some of these same issues I've mentioned.

Whenever I was really, really down, I could always go to the boy's dorm and ask for Paul. He was so such a good listener, never condemning, always gentle and kindhearted. He is my most special **blessing number twenty.**

To this day I know I could never have survived some of my trials if it wasn't for his kind friendship. I loved my brother Paul more than he could ever realize. Just having him there by me, listening, was such a comfort during some of my hardest trials. I praise God so much for my dear brother Paul, my most favorite blessing!

Chapter 4
The Happy High School Days

To my great disappointment, my brothers and I missed the grand escape of Dalat School from the approaching Viet Cong Communist rebels, bringing bombing very close to Dalat School. All of the MKs were frightened. The school moved to Bangkok while we were in the US.

Our denomination required missionaries to take a furlough after four to five years of service in a foreign nation. Therefore, I was in America during "The Big Dalat School Escape" because of the Vietnam War.

People in America have no idea the blessings they have in their country. MKs longed to go to malls or eat at McDonald's, because back then these franchises had not yet gone to the far ends of the earth, like Viet Nam and Thailand. MKs longed to dress cool, wear the latest hairstyle, learn new slang words, and watch TV shows.

Because of the lack of real self-worth, many MKs fell prey to copying some very unbiblical life styles while on furlough with their parents. I know this is true because of the temptations I gave in to, when I went back to the good ol' USA.

Our denomination required the husband to be away from their furlough homes for two to three months each in the fall and spring to speak at churches. I wish there had been a better way than to take the fathers away from their families during this period of time that brings the greatest of temptations to the children and an added strain on mothers without the support of husbands during this strategic time in a child's upbringing. I know most missionaries endeavor to be a "bond slave" of our Lord and Savior Jesus Christ by trusting and praying for God to protect their children while on furlough. Before God, my parent's intentions were pure and their hearts were true and clean.

On our furlough in Buffalo, New York, I fell into many and various temptations. I learned to dance to the music of the Beach Boys and The Monkeys. My dear mother prayed hard for me. I know because I heard her many times very early in the morning.

It was during this time on furlough, on the way home from school that I tried smoking my first (and only) cigarette in the bathroom of a gas station. It was totally awful and made me very sick to my stomach. I hated it!

My mother had spent her early years in Buffalo. She came from good solid Polish stock, and most of my classmates had Polish last names.

I can remember one kid, Brian Rozanski, who talked back to the teachers so much and made one of the teachers, to the whole class's amusement, break her pointer when she banged it on the desk!

Besides this, everyone cheated on tests. They would lay out their notebooks on the floor next to their desks with the answer pages open, and bend their heads to see it while taking tests. I never did this but I couldn't see why the teacher never did anything about it. I am certain that she saw what the students were doing.

I became very rebellious in my heart. My mother segregated me from any social event, even those connected to our church. For example, I was not allowed to go to an adult-chaperoned Youth For Christ Rally. It may be that, by God's wonderful design, because of her intervention I probably was kept from getting into more trouble!

Following the example of my friends, I even once stole pink pearl earrings from a store, and copied friends who would stuff their pockets full of candy from the small grocery store near the school. I have since written to the store and sent money including interest to repay what I stole.

But what I observed (using myself as an example) is that having fathers gone for several months at a time to speak in churches hurt students from Dalat School. It caused problems when the students returned from furlough and brought back with them many very evil and wrong influences.

After furlough, my younger brother and I returned to Dalat School, which was now in Bangkok, Thailand. I tried to get my MK roommates to learn to dance to rock music. I remember one all-night party we girls had in which I danced on a short decorative wall.

One of us that night had the idea to go scare the boys who were having an all-night party at the same time. We didn't do anything bad, but just tried to cause mischief. I am certain I saddened many of my dear dorm parents!

One day a friend and I got all dolled up and went for an adventure—an adventure that could have turned into a dangerous mistake. We had this curiosity about ships because we had traveled to America on ships, so we went down to the docks where huge ocean liners and cargo ships were lining the harbor. We gazed in wonder as we, two naive ninth graders, took an adventurous walk around the docks, all decked out like "spring chickens." The eyes of men followed us.

I know God's hand was upon us because after a couple of hours of watching the big ships, we got in a taxi unharmed and returned back to our Dalat School campus. **Blessing number twenty-one** is God's merciful protection while doing stupid things like two young American girls taking a walk alone along the Bangkok shipping docks.

Also that year during rainy season, the "klongs" (waterways similar to Venice, Italy) overflowed. You would understand the devastation this caused all over Bangkok when one realizes that Bangkok is called "The Venice of Asia." The entire city is lined with water canals.

I believe everyone prayed to keep us from illness as we walked through the filthy "klong" water. We had to use rubber flip-flops to get to and from classes. At the time I enjoyed the refreshing coolness of the water on my feet, and walking through six inches of water just to get to class was an adventure to me. In my mind it was exciting because it was just something different to kill the boredom I so often felt at this stage in my life.

Blessing number twenty-two came when God answered prayer by changing my life through the events of a course of a year. God used some rather unusual trials in my life to get my attention to show my need of Him.

The first one was a talent show in which I decided to quote and dramatize from memory William Shakespeare's, "The Seven Stages of Life," a piece of dramatization I had seen done by a professional actor at my school while on furlough. I had worked to perfect my piece—but getting up and performing before everyone was a different story.

I remember starting with a good loud voice and with some good dramatization, beginning with the first lines:

All the world's a stage,
And all the men and women merely players;
They have their exits and their entrances,
And one man in his time plays many parts,
his acts being seven ages. At first, the infant,
mewling and puking in the nurse's arms....

Suddenly my mind went totally blank. I walked off the stage and fled to my room where I cried for hours!

The second thing God used to bring me to Himself was that year I failed Algebra One. Now I knew for certain I was dumb! I remember I could not look at anyone in the face or even talk to anyone because of failing Algebra One. I felt like a psychological misfit—but God wasn't finished with me!

My rebelliousness extended to doing a very willful act while on vacation. A girl who was the daughter of an American government official living in Vientiane was my best friend. I liked her for her interest in philosophy and willingness to loan me books. One was a book by Hermann Hesse entitled *Demian,* written in 1919. It was a story about a boy named Sinclair. In the book Sinclair has a childhood friend and mentor named Demian who taught Sinclair that Cain was better than Abel because he stood bravely alone, accepting himself. Demian taught Sinclair self-realization. The major theme of the book is the existence of opposing forces and the idea that both are necessary. This intellectual book allowed me to compare Christianity with atheism. It was interesting and an eye opener to me!

At the same time my mother gave me the book entitled *In Cold Blood,* by Truman Capote. This is a book about what was going through a killer's mind as to why he found meaning out of killing people. These books caused me to rethink what I truly believed.

My US government friend invited me to a high school dance where the US Military lived. The question was how was I to get there without my parents knowing—of course I knew they would say no if I asked!

It happened that a fellow classmate from South Laos was staying with us while on vacation and was sharing my bedroom. I thought of a brilliant plan. My friend would drop one of my shirts out of the window. If I left and was caught, I could say I was going out to get the garment that had fallen on the ground. It was an adventure, and I am not proud of it. It was totally stupid at the age of 15 to catch a cab alone at ten o'clock in the busy nightlife of Vientiane, Laos, just to go to a high school dance. Did I enjoy myself at the dance? *No.* Did I have a deep down feeling of discontent? *Yes!* Did God protect me from any evil? *Absolutely!* Because God had great plans to use me for His kingdom in my college and adult years!

It was soon determined that Dalat School in Bangkok was not the most ideal place for Dalat School because of the temptations of the city and the crowded dorm rooms. It was decided to move the entire school to the highlands of Malaysia.

Travel to Dalat School in Malaysia was a kaleidoscope of interesting travel. From Vientiane, Laos, the journey went like this—first all the Laotian MKs would pile their luggage and themselves into taxis, which would take them to the border of Laos and Thailand, separated by the

Mekong River. To get across to Thailand, we went through customs, dragging all our suitcases onto a ferry boat where we crossed over to the Thailand side. After going through customs again, we then piled all our suitcases and ourselves into three-wheeled bicycles with covered seats in the back. I'm sure it was interesting to see twenty three-wheeled bicycles snaking their way, with all us white children and all our luggage, to the train station where we took an overnight train ride to the Bangkok Airport.

The overnight train ride was rather like a party, although it was still painful as we had just said goodbye to our parents. One or two adults always chaperoned us on the trip. We would hang out the window at each town train station all the way down to Bangkok and buy yummy Thai food from the vendors gathered around our train windows.

My favorite was spicy barbecued chicken on bamboo sticks. Just thinking of the taste now makes my mouth water. It was a long trip, but we were able to sleep by pulling down overhead beds, which were surrounded by curtains.

The bathrooms were a different story. None of the commodes worked—ever in our many trips back and forth to Dalat School. The floor was always covered with three inches of toilet water and urine because every toilet on the train was plugged up. MKs are made of tough stuff and we endured what we had to do without complaining.

At the Bangkok Airport was a train station where we would pick up our suitcases and walk over to the Bangkok International Airport. There we met up with more MKs. These MKs were from Thailand. After customs we boarded the beautiful Thai International jet. I believe the whole jet plane was filled with just MKs.

Some of the younger MKs would be crying as they had just said goodbye to their dear fathers and mothers. The lovely stewardesses would try their best to cheer them. Often all of us would sing during the flight—hymns, songs, and choruses. The stewardesses loved us and would hand out delicious cheeses from Switzerland.

When we landed in Penang, Malaysia we began the arduous voyage by bus up the mountains to Tanah Rata, which was where our new school was located. Woe to you if you were in the second or third bus because the diesel fumes from the bus in front was nauseating. What was even worse was that during the last three hours there were sharp hairpin turns before arriving at Tanah Rata. By then almost all of the MKs would have thrown up! Woe to you if your window was down because most of the vomit going out of the bus window from the person in front of you came back through the open window behind it!

So sadness, sorrow, and pain typified the beginning of the semesters of my high school years at Dalat School. But God had many exciting things in store for me!

I believe people were praying for me. **Blessing number twenty-three** was the spiritual influences in my life—answered prayer by loving people praying for me and special, godly preachers who came to speak to our Dalat School student body each semester.

I believe my life changed during the last semester of grade nine. I remember asking my friend (the one who had been so mean in my early years) to take a walk with me. On that walk I asked her how I could be a better person. She responded to me that I should be more disciplined.

A very, very fun and exciting thing also happened to me with my new friend who had at one time treated me with rolling eyes and ignoring me. Eventually we became very good friends. She asked me to help her do a report on Catholicism for a class. Her plan was to gain information by attending a Catholic mass. My friend had a marvelous sense of humor, or else we both must have been very, very tired, because I remember we sat in the back and giggled throughout the mass. However, I was happy that she received excellent marks on her paper for the class!

I learned through this period of my life that one's past will develop one for good and for the best, if one trusts God and submits to Him by the persevering grace that God provides. I was reminded of Joseph's response in Genesis 50:20, after all his suffering caused by his brothers' jealousy when they sold him to slave traders. Then while in Egypt, Joseph was falsely accused and sent to prison. The story ends with Joseph becoming second in command under Pharaoh. After all these events, Joseph reflected, "As for you, you meant evil against me, but God meant it for good."

God gave me grace to try and work on my looks, my grades, and to reach out to encourage others who were hurting. All of my habits from the US were gone, and instead I began to daily read my Bible and pray. I began to gain many, many friends. My parents were praying for me and in so many ways showed their love to me.

Though we now were in high school in Malaysia, our new family home was moved from Sayaboury, Laos to the capital city of Vientiane.

This move was because Dad was appointed field chairman.

I remember my brother Paul and I were so disappointed to no longer be in our old home of Sayaboury, next to the jungles of northeast Laos. We did not like the city of Vientiane because it was so noisy and filled with filthy diesel fumes and sewers.

But we would still take bike rides alone in Vientiane. Back then it was still safe. It was nice, but just not the same as seeing the beautiful rice paddies and distant mountains while riding our bikes in Sayaboury, which we still considered our real home town.

My mother was very outgoing and dogmatic. She was never afraid of voicing her opinion. She was always telling me how I didn't have any backbone. This was most painful. I was told to never loan out any of my necklaces or clothing, but I could never say "no" to anyone because of fear of bullying.

Whereupon the time came to open the suitcase after coming home from Dalat School, I knew I was going to receive an angry scolding from my mother for lost jewelry and torn or missing clothes. How I would cry and cry over those lectures.

When my brother Paul and I were around

eight we had the most miserable time, often at the dinner table. You can be thankful for the wonderful tender steak and roast beef we enjoy in America, because water buffalo meat is tough like shoe leather and impossible to swallow. My mother would become so angry waiting for us to finish eating, that she would quick as a flash, grab our mouths, force them open, and shove her finger to push the dried out hard piece of water buffalo meat down our throats.

She was quick to tell me that I did not have her shapely slender legs and that my short fat legs came from the "Tubbs" side; or that I had a bad complexion—not like her pretty olive skin.

On many occasions she was totally out of control with her anger because of something I did. When she was that angry I was pulled by my ears and hair into the bedroom for a whipping with a leather strap (without the buckle). I don't remember the cause, but I remember being pulled by my ears and hair while being shouted at all the way to my bedroom.

I have since learned that my mother grew up under the most tragic and sorrowful upbringing. Her father would beat her mother in a drunken fit. There are also other dark secrets in my mother's family that are so disturbing I cannot even mention them. I know I never could have gone through the painful childhood she went through. I understand now why she was like this, and of course I still loved her so very much!

About the time my Mom was eight years old, God brought an evangelist to visit in her mother's home in Buffalo, New York. I believe that because of the legalism of the Catholic Church and the fact that the entire family had suffered from so many things that Catholicism had never solved, God had already prepared their hearts. God intervened in the Kowles family by bringing this evangelist, who preached to the entire family. He told about true salvation through trusting only in the substitutionary death of Jesus Christ as the one who took their punishment for sin; and that only by trusting Jesus who suffered, died, and came back to life for each of them could they have their sins taken away forever. My mother's father became a Christian much later and died. It was after this when my Mother was 13 years old that the whole family gave away all their material possessions and moved to China as missionaries during the Depression.

I tell all this background because there is often a reason why people do what they do and say the things they do. I learned early to accept and say that I was wrong to my mother because

I loved her. I believe I understood my mother in a small way, so I loved her and I loved my dad both the same.

But parents all have faults to one degree or another and there were many things I appreciated and admired in my dear mother and father. I know that my parents always said they were sorry after disagreements and would make up and kiss and hug. My mother loved my father with all of her heart and my dad couldn't have been prouder of his dear outgoing wife with her engaging smile.

He loved her so very much until the last breath she took on April 2, 2013. My father stayed beside her day and night for a week holding her hand and telling her how much he loved her up until the very end. He never left except for a quick trip home to clean up, etc. In truth it was a day of rejoicing for all of us who came to be with my dear mother during her last hours on this earth, to know that when she drew her final breath she was in the presence of her dear loving Heavenly Father! What a glorious day of celebration it must have been for her!

I am very proud of my mother. I know she loved me, although she did struggle at times with the same sinful nature we all have. While in the little girl doll stage (which was when I was eight years and under), my mother sewed beautiful doll clothes for my dolls. I still have the dolls and doll clothes and treasure them, remembering my sweet mother's love and patience to sew them for me! They were beautiful clothes and in my little girl dreams, I was one of my dolls. I would use pretty hankies for sofas and decorate match-boxes and pretend my life was actually that of a real princess with bedrooms as large as a gym, lined with brocade couches, silk tapestries and lacy canopies, and large ruffled beds. In my imagination, beautiful, rich paintings lined the walls and lovely chandeliers with crystal globes hung in my bedroom.

One of my mother's gifts to me later in my teen years was her willingness to teach me to sew my own clothes. She encouraged me that I could do it, and do it well. Consequently we took many trips together to Bangkok where we bought Simplicity patterns so I could sew my own clothes.

Back in Vientiane, Laos I'd hop on my bike and peddle down to the Indian cloth dealers in the morning market to buy cloth. Those Indian sellers knew how to sell anything. They would follow me around as I was trying to decide what fabric to buy, saying, "Best price! Best price!" And then of course, after I chose the fabric, I would try to get them to lower the price a little. What an exciting experience it was to turn out collections of designer fashion outfits. With my artistic background I could turn out the most fantastic wardrobe.

My clothes turned many heads at Dalat School so that I was known as being very well dressed. Sewing is work. While on vacation, instead of wasting time, I learned to work by sewing. Diligent work brings profit. Proverbs 10:4, "A slack hand causes poverty, but the hand of the diligent makes rich."

Blessing number twenty-four is for my persistent mother who believed in me and didn't allow for self-pity to rule my life. As she herself overcame many obstacles in her life, she knew how self-pity could wreck a person's life.

I heard Elizabeth Elliot once say that she sometimes thought that the root of self-pity is a demon. Self-pity is so tricky because really its cause is pride. But Satan whispers we are worthless and pride tells us we are wounded by somebody and therefore must punish ourselves for being less than perfect. This sounds very much like a good dose of self-pride!

I was still very shy and insecure. One of my MK friends invited me to try out for cheerleading. I knew I would not be able to be a cheerleader without flubbing up somehow. But I prayed very hard for God to help me with my nervousness and insecurities. To my utter amazement, God strengthened my courage in the tryouts and I did quite well! I was accepted on the Dalat School cheerleading squad.

How much fun it was to go to the local schools all around Tanah Rata to cheer our basketball players. Some of the teams we played did not like the West and consequently our team, and we the cheerleaders, had tomatoes and other rotten things thrown at us. But I thought all of this political stuff was so exciting—another adventure!

A real and dangerous adventure came when one sunny Saturday in Tanah Rata about sixty kids and five adults went on an all-day hike in the jungles. It would have been wonderful, except we got totally lost miles in the deepest and darkest of jungles! Our guides lost their way!

Actually, the fact of people getting lost in the jungles around Tanah Rata was quite a regular occurrence, so you can imagine how we felt.

Just a year before, a millionaire businessman from Bangkok, Thailand came to Tanah Rata, Malaysia for vacation. He went out alone to hike and got lost. Many Dalat School upper class men and adult men took turns going with tribal guides to find this man. People searched for weeks but he was never found.

Our own primary school teacher, Miss Lang, used to go out to visit tribal friends with whom she shared the gospel. How sad it was to hear the news that she could not be found. Search parties went out day after day. I can only imagine how frightened she must have been and how hard she must have prayed. She was found after one week of searching. She was very weak but otherwise had no other problems. God answered so many prayers for her safe return.

These stories were on our minds as we waited and prayed to find our way back. Here we were, 60 school children and five adults lost in the deepest jungles, known to be inhabited by tigers. I can still remember several of us gathering in small groups to pray. Some of the younger children were crying. The sun began to go down.

Jungles in Malaysia are not like any jungles you've seen—except maybe much like jungles in the Amazon. The jungles are so thick there is absolutely no way one could go off the trail. But because there are many tribal people living in the jungles there are many small trails that crisscross all over, and one might actually be walking in a giant circle and never get anywhere—sort of like the giant mazes people make today out of corn fields. Only here in these jungles are the added dangers of real tigers and giant pythons, etc.

All the adults and children gathered in groups to pray for God to help us find our way out of the jungle. Through the mercy of God and the persistence of those brave jungle guides who hacked their way through the vines, we were miraculously saved. This makes **blessing number twenty-five**—saved from death by many prayers!

I can still remember the joy and relief I felt to arrive on an actual paved road on which we made our way back to our Dalat School.

Around grade ten a very terrible and almost tragic thing happened. Tanah Rata was the rest and relaxation place for Australian and New Zealand military guys. Seeing all these cute and sweet MK girls hanging around our Dalat School property drew many of these men to get acquainted with us.

But tragedy almost struck when one of the men who was dead drunk made it into the girls dorm and into my room where six of us lived. I was on the top bunk. I remember some noises that woke me up and then one of my roommates began screaming!

There I saw this drunken guy, half undressed

and trying to get into bed with my roommate! We were all terrified! This is **blessing number twenty-six!** God saved six MK girls from near disaster.

I know that God heard the prayers of parents and churches back in America who prayed faithfully for all of the staff, faculty and students of Dalat School. God answered prayers by bringing about 60 lost children safely out of the jungle! It was God who gave those Malaysian guides wisdom to know how to get us out of the jungles. God also answered prayer by shielding a pretty MK from an evil man intent upon doing a dastardly, very harmful deed to one of my dearest of roommates! What a wonderful, loving Heavenly Father we have!

Just like any high school, Dalat School had its favorite student hangout. In Tanah Rata, it was the Indian restaurant, which served chapattis with curry or sugar and sweetened condensed milk. All of us kids were best friends with the Indian owner and were very trusted, so all we had to do was go in, sign our name, and at the end of the year our parents would pay the bill.

I was always on a diet and weighed about 92 pounds so I didn't go often to the Indian restaurant. I felt proud that our school of American kids loved people and the delicious foods of many cultures.

Over my high school years I heard comments many times by people who would remark that MKs were very irresponsible. In the dorm room I remember discussions about this accusation and the conclusion was that we were like that because, since six years old, nothing at school really belonged to us. It belonged to the school.

Our attitude was that if anything was broken, someone else would pay to fix it. I think that it is true, but this was being irresponsible. Not thinking of where the money was coming from, some students would rack up big bills at the Indian restaurant.

One morning during a regular school day we saw the most amazing and funny thing! All schools have kids who like to pull pranks and this prank was pulled by some of them. During the night, some MKs took the school van, picked it up, and put it in the middle of the fountain located in front of the main building.

I think that although some of us caused them much grief, there was a feeling of real, genuine love coming from our dorm parents. We idolized them in many ways.

Chapter 5
Sayaboury, Laos—My Real Hometown

We were separated from our parents nine months out of every year. This was broken up by Christmas vacation and then summer vacation during the months of June and July.

As was previously mentioned, we were the only white people living in Sayaboury. In my mind I never felt any different from the Laotians. I admired many of the Laotian ladies for their great beauty and gracefulness. Their sarong calf-length slender skirts were feminine. Also they reminded me of ballerinas with their thick black luxurious hair pulled back in a stylish bun.

When I was just three, I remember our family was invited to a party at the governor's house. Oh, how I loved these events because it was a chance to watch the beautiful ladies dance the folk dances of Laos. After watching quite a few of the dances at events, I longed to learn how to dance.

At the age of four or five, the governor's wife

came to visit my mother. She was beautiful to me. Her nails were beautifully manicured and painted red. I was totally delighted when she offered to give me Laotian dancing lessons. But to my dismay, my dear mother declined—she thought it was too worldly. Although I never had a lesson, I caught on very quickly and could imitate the dance movements.

I consider this learning of a different culture a very great blessing. It will be **blessing number twenty-seven.**

Living in a place like Sayaboury, we learned quickly to not mind being stared at all the time. Often during Christmas break we took evangelistic trips to the nearest tribal villages. My brother and I were gingerly touched and the people would talk about us in the tribal or Laotian language, as they had never seen or felt white skin. Our hair was always commented on and touched, too.

We learned to not mind letting them touch us if they wanted. I can still remember the Laotian words meaning, "Your hair is very beautiful." Phonetically it would sound like this, "Pome Gham Dee Lie," translated literally, "hair beautiful very much."

Christmas was always the busiest time for evangelism with my family. The best trip was when we once stayed several days, sleeping at night in our Willy's Jeep, in a tiny primitive village called Nam Hia. Every family in the tribal village loved my parents and wanted to show their hospitality. About 12 families lived in this village. Every family invited us over for a large meal. It would often be mustard greens in a soup eaten with steamed sticky rice, which one could roll up in a ball like a piece of dough. There are no words to describe how delicious those dishes were.

The only trouble was, since we were there only a short time and every family wanted us over, we ate twelve meals in one day! It was very insulting to these tribal people to refuse to eat the food they prepared for us. Talk about being stuffed!

I believe to this day that the Asian culture all over Southeast Asia and China outdoes Americans one thousand to one in showing genuine hospitality and sheer excitement at having guests in their homes. Americans could take lessons from Asian hospitality, but Americans are too busy making money and enjoying their leisure.

The main purpose of the trips was to draw a crowd by showing Moody Science Films. Often they would have pictures of snow. The tribal people had never seen snow. Their way of showing amazement was the sound of "Tzh," repeated over and over again. This sound is made with the tip of the tongue behind the top teeth. The whole village would say this expression. Soon we also picked up this tribal habit.

After the film the Christians in the village would put on a Christmas play and then my dad would give an evangelistic message. It was a privilege to see these dear people who had lived in constant fear of evil spirits trust in the one true living God, who has power over death and the devil and evil spirits. How wonderful to see the huge mountains of fetishes on fire as the people destroyed these objects used to ward off evil spirits, which had kept them in bondage so many, many years.

Part of the excitement of these trips was the actual trip, which would often take all day, arriving at our destination after dark. This would be fine except our Jeep did not have doors, and it was common knowledge that the jungles were full of tigers. I was often afraid but would pray for dear Jesus to protect us.

One story of God's protection was while my parents were in language study in the town of Luang Prabang. I was about two at the time and I was preparing a pretend tea party for my brother Paul. To my dismay Mother took him inside for a nap so there I was still pretending in my own little world.

All of a sudden I noticed something that was shiny and beautiful! I wanted to get it out of the wall to look at it. I found a nice little stick about five inches long and tried to poke the shiny thing out, but nothing happened. I got the bright idea of how to get it out by going to ask my mother.

Wow! Did she ever move like lightning! She gathered me up as quick as a flash behind the folding French style doors where we watched as three Bible school students began smashing the wall with great force as they extracted and cut the head off of a nine foot long King Cobra snake!

This was recognized as a miracle of God's protection of me. How amazing it is to me to this day of how close I came to death by poking at this deadly snake for five minutes! We knew people in America were praying for us. In Luang Prabang there was no treatment for a deadly cobra bite. This comes to **blessing number twenty-eight**—thankfulness for the faithfulness of churches back in America praying for us.

As already noted, my parent's primary missionary work was in Sayaboury. They were the first foreigners to live there in this tiny town. My dad, with hired help, built our house out of wood, just like our next-door neighbor's house and many other houses up and down the street.

It was built about three feet up off the ground and was made of wood. The walls inside were the same as the walls on the outside. All the corner beams for the house were visible inside the house because the beams came up as high as the roof. My room beams were all painted bright pink and my brothers' room beams were painted turquoise.

Blessing number twenty-nine is having a talented dad who could repair a car, build a house, put in a septic system with a flush toilet, drill a well with pipes going up to a twenty foot water tower on which were two fifty-five gallon covered with a lids, and wire our entire house for electricity. A very antiquated generator provided our electricity (not like the ones seen today). It was run by kerosene. Dad was "Jack of all trades and master of them all." My dad also grew beautiful flowers all over our yard, raised chickens, and planted and harvested beautiful vegetables every year.

For many years we used kerosene lamps, an outdoor toilet hole in the ground, and hauled our own water just like everyone else in the neighborhood. Even my dear mother cooked on a raised, earthen cooking area over hot coals. She cooked this way even in the high tropical heat and humidity!

There were three cars consisting of Land Rovers or Jeeps in Sayaboury. The International Voluntary Service owned one vehicle, and the hospital, which was run by Filipinos, had the other car. In all the time I lived Sayaboury, I never saw a sedan car. Sayaboury did not have any traffic lights or electricity throughout the city except for the hospital and one or two other people's homes provided by generators. Most people traveled by foot, by horse, by wagons pulled by water buffalo, by bicycle, or by elephant.

How exciting it was when one of us would see an elephant coming, We would yell to everyone in the house, "An elephant is coming!" We would race to our fence by the road to watch the elephant slowly lumbering by, always with a man sitting on top, pulling logs or carrying large bags of rice, and even making deliveries to our neighbors.

Elephants, when untrained, are very destructive! One day an elephant came by with a smaller elephant. To get an elephant to work it had to go through arduous training to get it to be obedient to the owner. Evidently this smaller elephant had not yet been to training school because it stomped onto the neighbor's bamboo porch. Then after being chased out, it destroyed a bamboo basket in the yard. It was having a temper tantrum. We MKs have had the privilege of seeing so many interesting things and experiencing such a variety of unusual activities!

I was made to nap every day while living at home, especially if we were expecting to stay up late. I never could fall asleep quickly during nap time so to amuse myself I would play tricks on the ants going up and down the pink beam, just inches from my bed pillow. I saw they always used the same trail. I thought, *Hm-m-m, there must be a scent on that trail to keep them always going up and down in the same spot,* and so I would rub my thumb over several places.

Sure enough, when the ants came to those spots I rubbed, they lost their way and would wander all over the beam looking for that certain scent. It was a source of great amusement to me. It was always a surprise when someone would quietly come up and say, "Time to get up!" Upon awaking I realized I had fallen asleep while playing scientist with the ants.

Ants were always terrifying to me. These ants were on the beam by my bed, but I made sure my bed was far enough away so they could not get to me. Still they ate any piece of precious candy I saved. Even within a couple of minutes, they would be there swarming. These were black ants and did they ever have a stinging bite!

There was another kind of ant called the red ant. They lived in the grass and along pathways. What was terrifying about these ants was that they would crawl up to your ankle by the thousands before you knew they were there and then suddenly all bite at once. In a dead panic I would beat those things off my foot in seconds! To this day I am not real fond of ants.

A very sad tragedy occurred one vacation. There was an airplane that crashed just a mile from our airport. My dad and older brother, David were visiting a village nearby when they heard a very loud explosion and saw huge plumes of smoke billowing up in the sky. In a very big hurry they drove our Jeep to the airport and then walked to the crash site. It was a two-motor, propeller commercial airplane—the same kind of airplane we flew to boarding school.

A week later Dad took my brother Paul and me to see the crashed airplane. By then the charred bodies were removed. We collected items from the crash for souvenirs for my mom. They were the airplane glass caps over the ceiling lights. My mother used them as ashtrays for guests who visited us and who smoked cigarettes. I have one of those airplane glass covers in my home today. You can see the glass had melted from the fiery impact when it hit the ground.

It was a sad day for us however, as we contemplated on those who had died. I believe my dad had this in his mind as he sang a song we always sang when returning home on a trip. The song is a round and the title is "We're on the Homeward Trail." It is a song about how our earthly trail is really about our Heavenly trail.

Because my brother Paul and I had flown in so many airplane trips we had a fascination about airplanes and the airport. One of the most exciting things for us to do was to jump in our Jeep to catch the mail plane which we could hear coming. It was so exciting to go to the airport because then you saw interesting French people or maybe a person carrying a caged python or different kinds of monkeys!

Dad could speak French very well and would witness to the French pilots. Dad knew all the pilots by name. Going to the airport with my dad, for my brother and me, was an adventure. The trip just helped us feel like we were part of a bigger world.

My dad witnessed to the governor and many of the neighbors. My mom became known as "the doctor" in the neighborhood as one time when a neighbor came in complaining of terrible stomachaches, she treated him for a stomach ulcer and he was cured.

Any time of the day people would stop in to chat. The most interesting visitor was a man named "Boot Dee." Throughout each day Boot Dee would look at the beauty around him and wonder if there was a God.

One day he had a dream that a white man would tell him about God. Then someone told him that in the town of Sayaboury there now lived a white man, and he hurried to find my dad.

God's Holy Spirit broke into the darkness of Boot Dee's heart. How exciting it was for my dad to explain the whole plan of redemption starting from Genesis to Revelation. This story demonstrates the very true fact of Romans 1:20, "For His invisible attributes, namely, his eternal power and divine nature, have been clearly perceived, ever since the creation of the world, in the things that have been made. So they are without excuse."

Another time, my mom was out somewhere, and a man came to visit, so my brother Paul and I welcomed him in. We had small bamboo stools at our front door where we would all sit down to talk to our visitors. But this interesting tribal man was very curious about everything in our house, most especially the kerosene lamp.

I still remember him, kind of hunched over with his hands clasped behind his back, carefully tiptoe up to the lamp, bend down, all the while making noises, showing that he was very amazed!

He would walk slowly around the lamp peering up at the kerosene globe and then looking down into the glass cover. My brother Paul and I shouldn't have done this, but something about that cute old man's curiosity was so comical we could not stop laughing under our breath. The man never noticed us laughing because he was so overcome by seeing a kerosene lamp for the very first time in his life.

My parents would present the gospel to every visitor that came. Often ladies came in chewing betel nut (sort of like tobacco), but when they were done getting all the juice out, they didn't know what to do with the wad of betel nut. Near our front door was a knothole in the wood floor, with the ground three feet below that. You can guess where most often the wad of betel nut went!

One time my brother and I saw a lady put her wad of betel nut behind our kerosene-powered refrigerator. Up in the tribal communities, betel nut chewing was an addictive habit. It was terrible for the health of the person and all the teeth would turn totally black.

I praise God for the dedication of my parents because God used them to change the hearts of these dear Laotians and tribal people. It was the joy of my heart to see salvation brought to these people and therefore this is **blessing number thirty.** These people suffered from opium addiction, betel nut addiction, and alcohol addiction. Their fears were so great that evil spirits were in control to such an extent that they had to hire a witch doctor who would tell them to kill a chicken, put blood on different places in the house, and then hang wood images by the front door to chase away evil spirits.

Just to see and hear of so many people coming to trust Christ as their Savior through the ministry of my dear mother and dad was worth the heartaches I suffered at Dalat School!

Our family always showed an interest in the Laotian festivities. The time of the boat racing on the river was a wonderful cultural experience for us as MKs. The Lao men would race each other in very, very long slender boats, much like a canoe. It was sad in another way because so many used these festivals as a time for extreme drunkenness!

But the most memorable cultural event I experienced was when I was four years old, when the King of Laos visited our small village of Sayaboury. Everyone in Sayaboury dressed in the finest clothes they could buy or find. It was the most eventful ceremony my eyes had ever seen as the Laotian people of Sayaboury gave honor to their king. Laos is called "the land of a million elephants." Stretched as far as the eye could see were fifty elephants! Just as the king was ceremoniously seated all fifty of those elephants bowed their knees before the King of Laos.

My mother had dressed me in my one-and-only pink church dress. My parents were dressed as though they were going to an exquisite banquet. All the people in the village stood quietly in one long line down the street. It was an awesome experience. As the king slowly walked down, just two feet in front of each person, all the Laotians and tribal people would bow or kneel and he would speak a few kind words to them.

When he came to us he stopped also! We bowed low out of great respect to the king, not that he was god. No one said he was god. The king never said he was god either. It was just the cultural thing to do, to bow politely or even to kneel.

Finally he came to me, I smiled up as nicely

as I could and he smiled back and then warmly patted the top of my head. I'll never forget this awesome experience. This is **blessing number thirty-one**—the experience of the real king of our country paying little me such attention!

On another note, how more awesome it will be when we see our true Heavenly King some day in the future. That day will far surpass this in its glory and its majesty! Just to look into the eyes of the One who loved me so much, and gave His life for me, died on the cross, and came back to life so that I can live with Him forever will be truly awesome. As the wonderful hymn relates:

FACE TO FACE WITH CHRIST, MY SAVIOR
Carrie Elizabeth Ellis Breck/Grant Colfax Tullar
Public Domain

Face to face with Christ, my Savior,
Face to face—what will it be,
When with rapture I behold Him,
Jesus Christ Who died for me?

Refrain
Face to face I shall behold Him,
Far beyond the starry sky;
Face to face in all His glory,
I shall see Him by and by!

Only faintly now I see Him,
With the darkened veil between,
But a blessèd day is coming,
When His glory shall be seen.

Refrain

What rejoicing in His presence,
When are banished grief and pain;
When the crooked ways are straightened,
And the dark things shall be plain.

Refrain

Face to face—oh, blissful moment!
Face to face—to see and know;
Face to face with my Redeemer,
Jesus Christ Who loves me so.

Refrain

Heaven will be so wonderful. We can never imagine fully how wonderful it will be! This is why I am so blessed to be an MK. Just think of all the people I will meet in Heaven one day who were led to the Lord by my parents!

There are children in this world who suffer such evil, terrible things done to them. There is no place for me to complain, as God sees the awful evil done to all children. I was blessed with parents, though not perfect, just as I am not perfect and everyone in the world is not perfect.

I am so thankful to God for parents who cared enough to clothe me and feed me delicious food. When we came home from Dalat School, my dad and mom planned lots of fun family things to do together. Of all the things we did, I think the most important was that every day our family read the Bible and prayed together. This is **blessing number thirty-two.** Most people know this as family devotions. In this day and age, few families take the time ever to read God's Word and pray together! There's a saying which I believe is totally true and it is this, "The family that prays together stays together!" My dear husband Stephen and I continued this practice by having family devotions every evening with our son Samuel.

We did many other interesting things together in Sayaboury. I think the most unusual one was when Dave, my brainy five years older brother, came up with the bright idea of climbing the mountain five miles away with our father. When they got to the top they planned to catch a sunray on a large mirror they brought with them and shine them back to us, down in the village of

Sayaboury, using Morse code. Then my mother, Paul, and I would shine a large mirror back to them. I was about ten when we did this and it brought such a sense of togetherness and fun. It was so cool to think of my dad and big brother up on the jungle mountain with a mirror, and we were actually able to communicate to each other by Morse code. This is **blessing number thirty-three**—the blessing of having a clever and smart big brother! However, some of his cleverness was used as a way of manipulating my brother Paul and me to do things he wanted us to do, or not do things he didn't want us to do. He'd say, "OK, I was going to let you sit on my bed, but since you did that (whatever it was, I don't remember), I'm not going to let you sit on my bed."

David would use this kind of manipulation to force my brother and me to find and catch frogs for his snakes. Oh, yes, my brother David thought snakes were very cool.

Since we had devotions every night, we sometimes did something really different and fun during our devotions. We had a covered well for our running water, which my dad had put in with hired help. On many a starry night, we gathered on top of the well to sit and talk. Much of the time we studied the constellations and learned to find them in the sky.

After about an hour, Dad read the Bible using his flashlight and then we would all pray. Of all the things we did as a family, I think the most important was that every day our family would read the Bible together and pray together. This introduces **blessing number thirty-four**—the special quality times spent with my family.

Picnics were another favorite of ours. There were several favorite spots we enjoyed going to. One place was where there were these strange, naturally made volcanic-type black mounds or hills.

Our picnic food was often tuna fish and/or sardines with sticky rice dipped into spicy, garlic sauce. Yum!

Another day we all piled into our green Willy's Jeep. We found this delightful, grassy meadow, but just when we were getting ready to eat, it began to pour down rain. It really poured for a long time. But, I think, this was my most favorite picnic because we all just sat nice and cozy in our Jeep, perfectly dry, enjoying our sardines and sticky rice. Everyone was cracking jokes and my dad tells me that he remembers me saying, "Isn't this fun! We're all nice and cozy here!"

My dad can do just about anything, and do it very, very well. One of his best achievements in

Sayaboury was to bring okra to the local area from seeds sent from the States.

We had always a magnificent garden and our yard had many flowers, which my dad grew in beautiful quantities. We had gardenia bushes, fifteen feet tall poinsettias, bougainvillea, tiger lilies, hibiscus, and orchids. So **blessing number thirty-five** is the blessing of a lovely yard, bordered with so many beautiful flowers planted and nurtured by my dad. He truly blessed his wife and daughter by his "green thumb."

With all the work my dad did, where was his missionary work? Every Sunday I remember dressing in my best dress for church. The church service was held in a tiny, bamboo chapel, which my dad built next to our house. Every day neighbors were there, and also tribal people who had walked for three hours, just to get to our church to hear my dad preach the gospel.

Many times, Dad would take a guide and walk for weeks at a time, preaching at every village to which he was invited. So many of these villages, after hearing the gospel for the first time, burned all their fetishes which they used to appease the evil spirits.

It was often with great difficulty Dad reached some of these far-off villages. One of the worst trials were the blood sucking leeches, which would gather on his legs and even all the way up to his chest. After a trip his legs would be covered with sores from pulling off the leeches that got on him as he followed his guide through the mountain jungles of northeast Laos.

When he would arrive at a village, some of the villagers would run away from my dad out of fear. Dad would first meet the village chief and spend time with him. Then he would be invited to eat a meal.

Dad tells of the many meals he ate. The most "gourmet" was made out of monkey meat, and in the soup would be the monkey's hand. Here, my dad's humor would come out, when he would say, "But what I noticed was dirt under the monkey's finger nails." Dad would politely eat his soup.

After that, he would get out his pictorial scroll, telling the whole story of the Bible. They had never seen anything like this, so there were the sounds of amazement coming from all over the large crowd—"Tze! Tze!"

The house would be jammed with people, with even more people outside, peering through cracks in the bamboo walls, listening to my dad share the message of the gospel, from creation to stories about Jesus and then Jesus' death and resurrection.

There must be hundreds of people who trusted Christ through my mother and father's faithfulness to evangelize. These tribal people's religion was animism; that is, they believed in and were in constant fear of evil spirits, which they had to appease through an animal sacrifice or something similar.

I can still picture the many, many high fiery piles of burning fetishes the new believers burned. Their bondage to fear of the evil spirits was gone! They now believed in the true God who made the world and loved them enough to take their punishment for sins they had done. Now they had no fear of death or of evil spirits because God was more powerful than the evil spirits. They believed that one day they would live eternally in Heaven with Jesus Christ, who is now their God. This is one of my most precious blessings—**number thirty-six**!

In the late 1950s, in one such village far, far away, my dad was told a story that had been told each generation for hundreds of years. The story was that at one time, there was a great flood that covered the earth. No one in northeast Laos ever heard of radios at that time. They could never even understand what a radio was. So how did this very remote tribe know about a flood that covered the entire earth?

I say all this about my wonderful dad because he was a hard worker for the Lord. He poured out his life to reach people with the gospel, and also worked hard at home to make a wonderful home for his dear wife and children.

My dad had mostly German ancestry, which was why he was so diligent. I love my dad so much. He was always kind and patient to me.

My brothers and I had so many fun things to do in that lovely yard my dad cultivated. At night, my older brother David gave Paul and me lots of fun by chasing us with a flashlight under his face while making frightful faces. Paul and I would run laughing and screaming!

An exciting activity that brought a lot of fun into my brother Paul's and my life between the ages of ten and fourteen was to climb up the water tower where water was stored in fifty-five gallon drums. Water collected in the lids of the drums that provided our house with running water. Wow, did we ever have fun climbing all the way to the top, bringing with us caps for boats, stones to make pretend coves in a lake or ocean, and tiny branches for our tiny invented waterfront homes! We would float the caps across the drum lid and visit each other or take voyages exploring our tiny world. I still can't believe our mother let us do this!

It is only through the graciousness and tender mercies of our loving God that we never took a step backward. Only ten inches of standing space stood between a twenty-foot drop to the ground and us. Every once in a while Mom would come out on the back porch and yell, "Be careful children!" What an amazing God we had, who protected us as we enjoyed having invented fun on our vacation!

Playing tag was extra fun because our house was three feet off the ground. This added to the fun of chasing each other, as I could look under the house to see where my brothers were running. What child in America ever experienced the adventures we grew up enjoying every day?

We also had a net hung in our yard, and invited our Laotian neighbors over for badminton games. My parents witnessed to them and we always had many, many neighborhood people (especially children) come to our church for Sunday school and worship service.

After a large rain shower would pass through, my mother would let us go wading in our bare feet in the puddles all over the grass. I believe as children we were so very, very blessed by having Christian parents who did their best to provide for us and love us.

I think of so many kids who are on their second and third sets of parents. There is no way I, nor my brothers David or Paul, could ever complain. We had the best parents in the world!

Besides games, picnics, and races around our house, we had chores to do. My job was helping to wash clothes with the old-fashioned wringer washing machine. Then came the tedious job of pinning them up to the clothesline. I hated pinning clothes on the clothesline because the sun was so hot and bright, and my arms grew so very tired from holding them high up in the air. But I did it. I was also responsible to keep my room tidy and swept everyday.

My other job, which I really liked, was setting the table. Whenever I did this, I would try to invent in my mind what kind of lady I was. Then I would walk around the table pretending I was rich lady of etiquette. In my pretend world, I would imagine a handsome boy looking in the window and admiring me.

This brings me to the last blessing—**blessing number thirty-seven,** which just happens to be my brother, Paul's favorite number. This is the most wonderful blessing a parent can give their children and that is teaching them to work! A parent training their children to work is a lost art. Children will someday grow up, and if they weren't made to work while they were young, they will live mediocre lives. I am so thankful to God for giving me such godly parents, who taught me to work and to fear God!

Chapter 6
Why Does God Allow Us to Suffer?

Avocados! Yuck! They were all sliced up in the salad! What was I going to do? I remember, after being forced to take my first bite, my stomach began to churn! As an eight year old, I enjoyed eating most foods, even most vegetables, but these avocados tasted like what hair smells like! And the slices were slimy! I sinned that day by arguing vehemently with my mother. The Bible says in Colossians 3:20, "Children obey your parents in everything, for this pleases the Lord." Arguing is disobedience to God. Not only that, I hated my mother that day for making me eat it. She sent me to my room. In the room I gnashed my teeth in hate and without hesitation, promptly forced myself to throw up on my mother's handmade rose rug.

Now, I say about this my eight-year-old self, "You rebellious soul!" The one who hates in anger is a rebel against authority and most assuredly against God! I tell this story because some weeks later I asked Jesus to take my sins on the cross, knowing that I was a sinner.

It is good for all men to know that they are sinners as is everyone else in the world. As Romans 3:23 says, "For all have sinned and fall short of the glory of God." This explains why people do bad things, like hating, murdering, slandering others, lying, and adultery; and often we are the victims of their sin, such as jealousy.

It is only by God's mercy that we do not experience more pain. We all deserve worse because we are all sinners. Romans 3:12b says, "No one does good, not even one." We live in a whole world of people who are all sinners. But the fact is, that God is holy! It says in 1 John 1:5b, "God is light and in Him is no darkness [evil] at all."

The knowledge that I am a sinner and that all have sinned against God is good news to me because it explains why there are problems in marriages, friendships, and in life.

People who mistreat us are sinning against God. This knowledge has freed me so much so that, when I am ignored on purpose or slandered against, I just tell God on them! That all people are sinners explains why people bully others and do terrible evil things to others.

The Bible says in Romans 12:19, "Beloved, never avenge yourselves, but leave it to the wrath of God, for it is written 'Vengeance is mine, I will repay, says the Lord.'" God sees what people say and do to us.

Sin is rooted in self. When one will not admit they are a sinner and will not submit to God's laws, they are walking in rebellion against God and His Word, the Bible. If it weren't for God's great grace working in my life by giving me a strong guilty conscience, I probably would have gone away from God, which the Bible says leads to death and finally being forever separated from God!

We will never know why we suffer the evil done to us, but we do know that all people are sinners including ourselves. If we are unwilling to admit we are sinners and admit that everyone in the world are sinners, this means we are setting the rules for living and not allowing God to be in charge of our lives and other people's lives.

If we are setting the rules of how to live and not following what the Bible says, we are making ourselves out to be like a god. How powerful is a god-like self! A person like this has shrunk God down to a tiny human being! Who wants their god to be their self? God must be bigger, stronger, and able to love me enough to grab me (so to speak) by the nape of my neck and say, "Stop sinning! Sin hurts you and others! I love you! I died for you and took all your sin and the power to sin on myself 2,000 years ago!"

The whole world is fallen and under the power of sin. People are hurting. We suffer because of sin! The Bible in 2 Timothy 3:1-4 states, " . . . in the last days there will come times of difficulty. For people will be lovers of self, lovers of money, proud, arrogant, abusive, disobedient to their parents, ungrateful, unholy, heartless, unappeasable, slanderous, without self-control, brutal, not loving good, treacherous, reckless, swollen with conceit, lovers of pleasure rather than lovers of God." Doesn't this exactly describe people in our world today?

They are under such a great burden of guilt because of sin that they are trying to get rid of it by doing this good thing and that good thing or by taking vengeance on the nearest close by person!

The fact that everyone suffers to one degree or another, at one time or another in life, must leave no room for self-pity. The Bible calls Satan a liar in John 8:44b, "He [Satan] was a murderer from the beginning, and does not stand in the truth, because there is no truth in him. When he lies, he speaks out of his own character, for he is a liar and the father of lies."

One of Satan's tricks is self-pity. He whispers,

"You poor thing. You are all alone. No one really cares about you. Why don't you just run away?" Self-pity is so very dangerous and I believe it comes from the pit of Hell. It is the cause of overeating and every other addiction on the face of this planet, including shopping, drugs, pleasures, and laziness! It is actually caused by self-loathing. They feel so guilty that they hate themselves, and to ease the pain of shame and guilt, they turn to addictions.

The Bible teaches that Satan has no power but that which God allows. Of all the suffering that happens in the world, the first cause is God and the second cause is Satan. Out of God's sovereign will He allows Satan to touch humans and this earth with suffering and pain.

We will never know why tragic things happen. But in the book of Job in the Bible one can see the whole story of first cause and second cause. In the first chapter the Lord says to Satan, "'Have you considered my servant Job, that there is none like him on the earth, a blameless and upright man, who fears God and turns from evil?' Then Satan answered the Lord and said, 'Does Job fear God for no reason? Have you not put a hedge around him and his house and all that he has, on every side? . . . But stretch out your hand and touch all that he has, and he will curse you to your face.' And the Lord said to Satan, 'Behold, all that he has is in your hand. Only against him do not stretch out your hand'" (Job 1:8-11).

So Satan leaves and causes Job and all his family to lose their livestock by theft and fire; and lastly, Satan causes a strong wind to blow on the house in which all Job's children were eating and drinking and kills all of Job's children and their families.

Next in the panoply, God says to Satan, "'Have you considered my servant Job . . . He still holds fast his integrity, although you incited me against him to destroy him without reason.' Then Satan answered the Lord and said, 'Skin for skin! All that a man has he will give for his life. But stretch out your hand and touch his bone and his flesh, and he will curse you to your face.' And the Lord said to Satan, 'Behold he is in your hand; only spare his life'" (Job 2:3-6).

Satan then goes and strikes Job with horrible boils from the soles of his feet to the crown of his head. Job 2:10b, "In all this Job did not sin with his lips." In the same verse, Job said to his wife after she told him to curse God and die, "You speak as one of the foolish women would speak. Shall we receive good from God, and shall we not receive evil?"

In this story about Job we get some ideas on the whys of evil happening to the best people. The reasons for most of the tragic things that happen in this world we will never know until we get to Heaven.

I heard an excellent definition of suffering from Dr. Erwin W. Lutzer (Moody Church pastor located in Chicago). He said, "Suffering is having what you don't want. And suffering is not having what you want." I believe this to be the best and most conclusive statement about suffering.

People seek to meet their needs through sex, but after a while sex outside of marriage becomes boring so they turn to more and more depraved sexual acts. This downshift is often called "the Law of diminishing returns." The Bible says in James 1:15, "Then desire when it is fully conceived gives birth to sin and sin when it is fully grown brings forth death."

To answer this question about why God allows sin and suffering, we must first admit that we can never totally know God's ways. There are many evil things done to people of which we will not know why they have happened until we get to Heaven. I know of two people's testimonies that have helped me to trust God when God allows great terrible evil to happen to nice people.

The first testimony is that of Joni Erickson

Tada. Why did God allow a beautiful Christian girl to dive into a lake and break her neck so that she became a paraplegic for the rest of her life?

But those of us who have read her books know the influence Joni has had on people all over the world. Because she trusted that God loved her, in spite of being a paraplegic, Joni now has her own radio ministry and a conference ministry to reach out to the handicapped. She uses her beautiful voice to bless our lives. She uses her mouth to paint beautiful pictures. God has given Joni many, many talents and she uses them for the glory of God. Her story has ministered to thousands as they see one, who by example, believed that what was evil God meant for her good.

The second person is Dori Van Stone who was sexually molested for years. Dori trusted God and was willing to tell her story. Her story has helped thousands to trust God in spite of the heinous evil done to her. But why does God allow these kinds of tragic things to happen to people?

I bring all this up because at issue for me as an MK was, *Why me? Why am I the one God chose to be born to missionaries and sent to live hundreds of miles away from my parents?* These are hard questions that I am going to try to answer because my experience as an MK was very, very, emotionally painful! I hated it! But the experiences I've described in this book are not at all near the tragic things other Christians have had to trust God with, such as Dori or Joni! Their stories have so much helped me have the correct Biblical perspective on my emotionally painful past as an MK.

I have had to wrestle with these questions my entire life, and I have many verses to build my case—that GOD IS LOVE—even though very, very, awful and tragic things happen to Christians and to good people, such as Job in the Bible.

Joni Erickson Tada, Dori Van Stone, and Job stand as heroes who, like Christ, endured the "crosses" God gave them, despising the shame. They have been beacons of hope for millions who have suffered, to not give up but, to keep holding the torch of faith high!

Everywhere in the world today there are stories of people who suffer physically because they tell others of the great love God has for mankind by sending His only Son to die on the cross to free man from the internal guilt they feel, though some people sin so much that they don't feel any more guilt.

All over the world Christians can't help but speak of the love of Jesus Christ, in spite of the potential for being persecuted for their faith. Just a side note here, I often wonder what the world has against Jesus and the Bible, because in all that Jesus did, He was always compassionate, kind, and forgiving. Jesus touched the leprous person, He went out of His way to love the outcast, and He especially had compassion for parents who were losing their children through death. The only people He judged were the hypocritical religious Jewish leaders who "talked the talk but didn't walk the walk."

The true Christian believes Jesus was the substitute for us by taking on death, even Hell, and coming back to life. The true Christian cannot stop talking about how great the love of God is. As a result there are true Christians all over our world who endure suffering, torture, labor camps, and other heinous ways of suffering.

Elizabeth Elliot, writer and speaker whose first husband was murdered by an Auca Indian tribe in Ecuador while Elizabeth and her husband were endeavoring to bring the Gospel to this very remote, primitive tribe, says that out of her deepest sufferings she learned the deepest things of God. We can actually learn what God meant when He said in Hebrews 12:3-4, "Consider him [Jesus] who endured from sinners such hostility against himself, so that you may not grow weary or fainthearted. In your struggle against sin you have not yet resisted to the point of shedding your blood." It is glory to suffer because of the Cross, if we refuse to return evil for evil but instead, entrust ourselves to a faithful Creator in doing what is right.

By submitting to suffering, God teaches us deeper things about Himself. Corrie Ten Boom, who suffered in a Nazi concentration camp, said that, "Yet in the deepest suffering God goes with us deeper." This was so true in my own personal experience, while being taunted, isolated, and hated in boarding school.

In 1 Peter 1:6-7, God tells us that one purpose for enduring suffering is to show us that our faith is real. " . . . You have been grieved by various trials, so that the tested genuineness of your faith—more precious than gold that perishes though it is tested by fire—may be found to result in praise and glory and honor at the revelation of Jesus Christ."

At the time we suffer unjustly and trust God, we must believe that we have been given a blessing to help others in their suffering.

When I entrusted myself to God while enduring suffering at the hands of MKs at Dalat School, I often felt the smile of God's face looking down on me in approval because I was not willing to return evil for evil. The Bible says that it is God who takes revenge and it is not our job to pay back people with vicious words or hurt their property because we ourselves have been rejected or verbally attacked!

Unfortunately, another reason we suffer is because of our own disobedience to God's written Word. It says so clearly in Hebrews 12:5-11, "'My son, do not regard lightly the discipline of the Lord nor be weary when reproved by him. For the Lord disciplines the one he loves and chastens every son whom he receives.' It is for discipline that you have to endure. God is treating you as sons. For what son is there whom his father does not discipline? If you are left without discipline, in which all have participated, then you are illegitimate children and not sons. Besides this, we have had earthly fathers who disciplined us and we respected them. Shall we not much more be subject to the Father of spirits and live? For they disciplined us for a short time as it seemed best to them, but he disciplines us for our good, that we may share his holiness. For the moment all discipline seems painful rather than pleasant, but later it yields the peaceful fruit of righteousness to those who have been trained by it."

We suffer because of our own foolish sins. There was a rule at Dalat School that we were forbidden to write with pencil marks on the wood tops of our desks. I don't remember doing this much, but one day I was not actually writing on the desk but tracing above the imprinted writing. The Bible reminds us in 1 Thessalonians 5:22 to avoid the very appearance of evil. Clearly what I was doing was a bad example—it definitely appeared to others that I was breaking the rules. I never forgot the lesson I learned that day. What was my punishment? It was to match and fold all the boys' socks. It took me at least two hours to do this boring tedious job. So we do often suffer from our own willful, thoughtless decisions.

All those years of suffering at Dalat School seemed like thousands of years. There were times I dug my hands in the grass and sobbed, writhing in real pain, when all along God was drawing me ever closer to Himself. You see I was not fully obeying God, especially in self-discipline. I also needed to be reading God's Word the Bible every day and I certainly wasn't doing that. So we see that God often uses suffering to root out the sin in our own life and teach us that He still loves us. During those years the verse most often in my mind was Matthew 19:30, "But many who are first will be last and the last first." Learning to be humble and hunger after God at an early age is a great blessing from God!

When we do suffer for our own sins often pride will cause us to become angry at ourselves. We might become so angry that we retaliate in some way or even feel like taking our own life. This is pride in our hearts because we see that we are not as perfect as we thought. In truth this is the very epitome of a very selfish person. We think, *it is just my own person I am hurting,* but in reality we fail to remember all the people who are deeply grieved by taking our own life. Satan will whisper in our ear that we have done this terrible thing far too many times, that there is no hope to change for the better and therefore we must punish ourselves. We must remember that Jesus said of Satan in John 8:44, "For he is a liar and the father of lies."

It is encouraging to realize that many famous heroes of the faith in the Bible felt this way too, when Satan seemed to get the best of them. For example, in 1 Kings 19:4, Elijah went a day's journey into the wilderness and sat down under a broom tree. There he sat feeling discouraged that he had not done enough for the Lord. Elijah said, "It is enough; now, O Lord, take away my life, for I am no better than my fathers."

Peter was another. He promised Jesus in Luke 22:33, "Lord, I am ready to go with you both to prison and to death." Yet before the day was over Peter had denied Christ three times. When questioned by observers if he was a follower of Jesus, Peter replied all three times that he didn't even know Jesus. This caused Peter so much grief of heart that we read in Luke 22:62, "And he went out and wept bitterly.

While being insulted and put down by others, and as a result, a Christian chooses to hate others and perhaps God or themselves and even do physical harm or react negatively—a true Christian will feel a great sense of shame soon afterwards.

About the time I was nine years old I was playing with a friend and fell in love with her gorgeous thick head of hair. Being shy and having a lack of ability to express myself I said, "You have such a big head." In later years I felt such a deep shame over that comment because she understood me to say that she was very proud. I took this misunderstanding to Jesus and asked His forgiveness. From then on I felt such a cleansing of my guilty conscience for my thoughtless comment and my shame disappeared.

When we fail God through disobedience in thought, word, or deed, we should feel a sense of shame and deal with it by kneeling in humility and applying 1 John 1:9, "If we confess our sins, he is faithful and just to forgive us our sins and to cleanse us from all unrighteousness."

Whenever I fail God my first offense is against God, and if I have hurt anyone either verbally or physically, my second offense is against another human made in the image of God. Therefore, we should not do to others what we would not want them to do to us. Would we want someone to hurt ourselves verbally or physically?

Suffering always will come to all of us in one way or another. For the Christian, God is our Father who sometimes disciplines us and is always rooting out the sins deep in our heart, like pride and jealousy.

Satan hates humans who are made in the image of God. His desire is to destroy the human image of God. When one becomes God's child Satan becomes very angry and will try many temptations to get us to rule our own life without God in it. John 10:10 states that Satan comes to steal, kill, and destroy. Jesus said, "I came that they may have life and have it abundantly."

One time I listened to Satan by taking revenge. A person in a church where my husband was pastor told me that I was a big problem by doing too much in the church when the real problem was no one would or could teach the Bible to children. All that was done with kids was fun and games. So I told this woman off and got mad at her.

I know I am God's child because within an hour I was grieved in my heart at my prideful answer and hurtful cutting words to this lady. Revenge doesn't help in the least, rather it brought me great sorrow and tears for what I had said.

Often we suffer shame from sins which we have done it doesn't help to beat ourselves over the head, or try to cover what we did with good works. The only way to deal with suffering done to us or from mistakes which we have caused ourselves is to forgive others and to forgive ourselves, even if there might be consequences.

If we can't forgive others we are forgetting how much more we have sinned against God. In Ephesians 4:32, it says "Be kind one to another, tenderhearted, forgiving one another, as God in Christ forgave you."

When we can't forgive ourselves for our sins, we are making ourselves out to be God. God forgives us but we can't forgive ourselves. We are really saying that we have a higher standard than God does. In reality our heart is full of pride! As God's child, if we don't learn to forgive ourselves God will bring more suffering to root out the pride in our hearts and we will become self-centered, overly sensitive, always suspicious that others are against us, and overly critical of others and ourselves. The result will be that people will not enjoy being around us.

We may also suffer by mistakes either done inadvertently or out of negligence. One may suffer excruciatingly for this kind of trial.

One day I heard the most tragic news about something a dear Christian friend of mine had inadvertently or negligently done. It is a parents' worst nightmare. She got into her car, backed up to go to the store, and ran over her neighbor's son and killed him. I met many times with my friend following this tragic event. The counseling done by our pastor and my friend's own close walk with her dear Lord and Savior gave her the supernatural strength to walk through this real nightmare.

For many of us our mistakes, inadvertent or negligent, cause us to become depressed, very embarrassed, and angry at ourselves and/or God. We beat ourselves over the head and tell ourselves that we are so stupid. We cause our bodies to suffer physically and we don't think clearly because we are so upset with our stupid decision.

Some of my own mistakes have caused me to become depressed and angry at myself. One such example was as a result of a stupid choice.

I absolutely hate our new shed. It was my choice because the colors matched our house. But I failed to notice that the shape resembled a horse barn. This dumb choice cannot be changed, and it is an eyesore which depresses me every time I see it.

It is incorrect Biblical theology for me to carry on with such depression and feel mad at myself. First, God could have made me see that it looked like a horse barn, but all I saw were the matching colors. This kind of suffering about my problem does probably sound stupid to some, but how many become upset because of circumstances beyond our control or because of our negligence? Have you ever changed your hairstyle on a whim and realized afterwards that it was terribly unbecoming, and furthermore it would take time to grow it back? We do often suffer embarrassment for our own choices and feel silly as though everyone can see what a dumb decision we made.

People who have a great sense of humor have often observed that they became the class clown in order to cover the grief of suffering in their heart. From this we can see that for mild mistakes we should try to look at ourselves with a sense of humor. Proverbs 15:15 says, "All the days of the afflicted are evil, but the cheerful of heart has a continual feast."

The one person, in my opinion, who wins the prize for always having a cheerful heart in spite of all the disappointments in his life is my bother-in-law Paul Van Valkenburg. At the age of four he suffered from surgery caused by a very large tumor at the base of his skull. The results of the tumor and surgery 55 years ago has resulted in numerous problems for Paul. The amazing consequence is that in all the past 39 years that my family has spent with Paul, we have never heard one single complaint! Instead we hear a steady stream of funny jokes. In fact his pun jokes are so contagious that our own family enjoys cheering ourselves up by using funny puns.

One solution to this kind of suffering is to study the book of Job and choose to trust God that God is always the first cause and God sometimes allows Satan to be the second cause. We might never know the exact reason. In very tragic mistakes, such as the tragedy of my dear friend's accident of running over her neighbor's child, I would guess that the second cause is Satan. But for most of us, I suspect we suffer for our mistakes because God is disciplining us to root out the sin of pride for which we should be thankful. Most prideful people tend to put up a false front so everyone thinks they are perfect in every way even better than everyone else. The verse most fitting for this is Psalm 16:18, "Pride goes before destruction and a haughty spirit before a fall." But even then it may be that only in eternity we will finally see the entire tapestry of our lives instead of the tangles, and realize that God always meant good for us that which we thought was meant for evil.

Another way people suffer is that, when they look back on their lives, they can become very miserable and suffer for *if only I had done this!* or *if only I had not done that!* For example, when an individual loses lots of money because of a wrong financial choice. For years I have been haunted by a very, very, poor decision I made, that today, if I had not made this wrong choice, I might be quite wealthy, or at least still be enjoying my treasure.

One day I was given an original print of a wonderfully interesting Norman Rockwell painting. The print was two and a half feet wide by three feet tall of a soldier returning to his home in the city. The artist had painted a street background with five-story red brick buildings in it. What was so interesting were all the people welcoming him home—kids, grocery store owners, the shoe shine boy, the cotton candy seller, and others from the neighborhood—all coming out to welcome him with grins on their faces. People and neighbors, little old ladies, cute little girls, and grinning parents, were hanging out of the windows of the buildings waving hankies or the American flag. Even cute dogs and neighborhood kids were scampering along beside the soldier eager to meet again their long lost friend! It was such an interesting print. To this day I have never again seen a copy of the print, even in collections of Norman Rockwell's paintings.

I had just been married for about two years when I was given this print, and our job required so many, many moves across the United States. Besides this, I despise living in a junk-filled house full of stuff being saved. So after about four years of many times of moving and and carrying this print everywhere I threw it in the garbage. Many, many years later when my husband and I were ready to finally settle down and live in a permanent home is when I began to beat myself over the head about this painting! Why oh why did I ever do such a stupid thing like that! Besides I love the color red and it would have looked gorgeous in our kitchen or den!

Worry about this decision cost me lost sleep, extreme depression, feeling angry at myself, and numerous other ways of beating myself over the head about such a stupid decision! Finally over the years I have tried to get everything in the right perspective and realize that all the worry in the world can never bring back the painting. One way God helped me with this constant depression and suffering was to remind me of what is really important in life. What in our lives will last forever? The Bible teaches that the earth will one day pass away, but only God's Word will remain forever. In Matthew 24,35, Jesus is speaking, "Heaven and earth will pass away, but my words will not pass away." Also the Apostle Paul wrote in 2 Thessalonians about what is going to happen to those who are not a Christian. Paul writes in chapter 1, verses 8 and 9 that Jesus will come with His mighty angels "in flaming fire, inflicting vengeance on those who do not know God and on those who do not obey the gospel of our Lord Jesus. They will suffer the punishment of eternal destruction, away from the presence of the Lord and from the glory of his might." Wow! What is of most importance on this earth are not things, but God's Word and people. God's Word and people are going to last forever and ever and ever.

Worrying and making ourselves suffer because of *if only I had done this* or *if only I hadn't done that* shows that in our heart we are not trusting God that He could have made us make the right decision or made us avoid making a wrong decision. Often the root cause of this suffering from bad decisions is the sin of pride. When I think of the painting and think, "Boy, I could be wealthy by now, but I made this stupid decision," and suffer terrible depression as a result, the root cause is pride. It shows also that in my heart my real treasure was in money or the object, not in the gospel or in people. I ask myself, have I ever suffered lack of sleep because there are neighbors who are not saved or those who I know have wounded hearts?

I believe God allowed me to throw away the painting to cause me to have a trial of suffering depression and lack of sleep to show me my heart. I learned that I valued things and money more than God's Word or people's eternal destiny.

While at MK boarding school in Dalat School I suffered anger and great personal loss when someone stole from my "care package" sent to me from my parents. In the package was some delicious American candy. For months I suffered anger over that little bit of stolen candy. Even as a young ten-year old God was trying to teach me what was really important in life—but I failed to learn the lesson. I am thankful God is still teaching me to always try to see the loss of things from God's viewpoint, to teach me what is truly important in life!

Did you ever wonder why it mentions in Revelation 21:4 that some people will be crying in Heaven? Heaven is a wonderful place, why will there be tears? I think I know why! We just might be having some of those "if only" kind of situations come into our thinking, which causes suffering. *If only* I hadn't spend all my time shopping, spent so much time on this hobby, given all my years to climbing the corporate ladder, and hardly ever spent time telling people about the Cross of Jesus Christ. But there is such comfort in Revelation 21:3-4, "God himself will be with them as their God. He will wipe away every tear from their eyes." Aren't you so thankful to read about how tender and compassionate God is toward His children when we read this? We must never worry and suffer depression about bad choices involving money but change our hearts so that the real treasures of our hearts are God's eternal Word and human beings!!

Lastly, Christians endure suffering with patience show to the non Christian that Christians live for something real and tangible. This kind of suffering is so needed today as people in our world go from one spouse to another spouse, from one popular car to another popular car, and from one dress fashion to another to fill the void in their lives. Pascal, the famous philosopher, once said, "There's a God-shaped vacuum in the heart of every man which can only be filled by God who is Jesus Christ."

I recently read the unabridged *Les Miserables*, written by Victor Hugo, which beautifully tells how God uses suffering to bring good into the hearts of evil people.

The main character Jean Val Jean labored unjustly for twenty years in cruel hard labor. He was a man with a big void in his heart. He escaped and by a strange turn of events was invited to sleep and eat for the night in the home of a good priest.

In the night he left and stole the silver forks and knives. He was caught and was brought back to the priest. The merciful, forgiving priest (like our Father in Heaven) went in to the house, brought out two large silver candelabras and gave them to Jean Val Jean. The priest then told the police to free Jean Val Jean as he had already told Jean Val Jean that everything in his house was his. The forgiveness of the priest totally changed Jean Val Jean to do good the rest of his life.

Witness the example of those who endure suffering today, such as several Laotian pastors in prison, who gave away their one and only daily handful of rice to the other prisoners who were in prison for theft or murder. As a result, many of the criminals trusted Jesus Christ, who died to take the punishment that they really deserved, as their Savior.

This was love given by the Holy Spirit to demonstrate to the unbelieving world that God is real! When the world sees Christians endure suffering with patience, love, and peace, the Christian life becomes desirable. These Laotian pastors' sacrificial love for their neighbors demonstrated the most reliable witness of the veracity of the Bible. Those who reject God, reasoning that they have never seen God, forget that God has already shown us Himself in the person of Jesus Christ and in the lives of all true Christians.

Jesus forgave sins, just as God does, proving Himself to be God. Jesus had power over death, wind, storms, blindness, leprosy, and the demonic world. Jesus, who is God, really did take the punishment for our sins on Himself 2,000 years ago. It was His death and resurrection to life that was the substitute for us. He didn't just die as all of the other leaders of religions of the world, but Jesus willingly died—and proved He was God by predicting His own death on the Cross and coming back to life on the third day (prophecies which are recorded throughout the Bible). Eyewitnesses saw that Jesus was dead and then they saw Him alive!

If we suffer a lot, or if our suffering is tragic and heinous, the Bible says in Isaiah 45:6b-7, "I am the Lord, and there is no other. I form light and create darkness, I make well-being and create calamity, I am the Lord who does all these things."

We read stories of early Christians who suffered heinous deaths. Some were sawn in two. Others were burned as human torches to light the city of Rome.

Today a real story of martyrs is told about Christian persecution in Laos. Christian prisoners are put down into an earthen hole alone, with no room to even turn around. The air is hot and humid; ants crawl all over them and bite them. They are given a bag in which to defecate. These Christians testify that when they give the bag up to the guard, the guard will on purpose poke a hole in it so that all the terrible smelly, germ-filled contents will pour all over the Christian buried in the hole.

If the Christian is by chance released they will not stop talking about the wonderful truth of a wonderful God who sent His Son to save people from their sin, guilt, and shame. These Christians do not complain asking, "Why me?" To them it is their greatest joy to suffer for their Lord and Savior Jesus Christ! I believe this is why so many in the country of Laos are believing in Jesus as their Savior—that He did indeed die on the Cross for their sins. These Christians show that there is a real God and and for Him it is worth dying.

The only real truth in the entire world is God's Holy Word, the Bible. We must choose to believe with our will that God allows everything in our life. In Isaiah 45:9, "Woe to him who strives with him who formed him, a pot among earthen pots! Does the clay say to him who forms it, 'What are you making?'"

When we compare our sufferings with others we must still trust God, that we are loved! Deuteronomy 33:27a says, "The eternal God is your dwelling place, and underneath are the everlasting arms."

Run to God; pour out your grief and fears. In Psalm 62:8, God's Word says, "Trust in him at all times, O people; pour out your heart before him; God is a refuge for us." He is alive! He loves you! You are not alone in your suffering. Many, many others through out history have suffered in the same way and have refused to quit their life of walking in faith and trust in a loving God. They may not have ever known the reason on this earth why God brought the suffering but they still trusted. Job trusted God and said in Job 13:15, "Though he slay me, yet I will hope in [trust] him."

In 2 Chronicles 16:9, God has a message of comfort for those who suffer: "For the eyes of the Lord run to and fro throughout the whole earth, to give strong support to those whose heart is blameless toward him." During my hardships growing up, I often questioned God—but I always ended up choosing to believe that God was allowing the suffering for a good reason. I knew that I must choose to forgive others and to believe that God was pleased with me and that He loved me even though others did not.

Chapter 7
How to Have Victory Over Bullying and Rejection

God gave us rules to follow on how to have peace with our neighbors, our parents, our brothers/sisters, our children, our husbands/wives, and ourselves. God said the greatest commandment, found in Matthew 22:37 and other places in the Gospels is, "You shall love the Lord your God with all your heart and with all your soul and with all your mind."

This is the first rule. If we disobey God in this we will never have peace with ourselves, our neighbors, those we work with, or our families because the Bible says in 1 John 4:7-8, "Beloved, let us love one another, for love is from God, and whoever loves has been born of God and knows God. Anyone who does not love does not know God, because God is love."

God is love. We learn how to love by knowing God through reading His Word the Bible. If we do not read God's Word daily we will not learn to love others as we should. The result will be arguments, conflicts, frustrations, and lack of peace.

The second commandment after this is found in Matthew 22:39, "And a second [commandment] is like it: You shall love your neighbor as yourself." There's an old Indian saying, "Never criticize your neighbor until you walk a mile in his moccasins." This means we criticize because of bias or false assumptions because we don't know the person well enough.

One day several years ago I was picking up an order of glass for a picture frame. The receptionist was unreasonably irritable. I immediately took it personally, wondering what it was about me she didn't like. Before I responded with a sharp answer, I wondered if maybe she had some inner problem. So I tried a test. I asked her how her day was going. To my surprise she responded by saying she had been on the phone with her ex-husband and was really hurting. God gave me a powerful lesson that day.

I think store clerks in particular suffer because customers are grumpy and criticizing. But we must realize that all are suffering—the customers and the clerks. The world looks highly on people who act confident, look well dressed, have nice facial features, are well mannered, and have a good sense of social etiquette. People today put on a false front so that they appear successful. If you were to look into their hearts you might see a man with a heart in pain because he was sexually abused by his father as a child, or a woman who feels guilty all the time because of an abortion or perhaps explicit sexual acts done at some time in her life. The result is broken homes, suicide attempts, financial losses, untimely deaths, quarreling in the neighborhood, etc.

We must believe that people have deep wounds that never go away. Those who do not have a personal relationship with God cannot love others as they should and as a consequence, they retaliate by mistreating others. Our job is to forgive and to tell God on them.

The Christian who reads his Bible faithfully knows that God always wants us to know that He is in charge and whatever is done to us is because of His hand of love and mercy. Though on this earth we may not understand the whys of suffering, the Bible is full of promises of God's special love for those who suffer patiently, trusting in a God who sees the whole picture!

Following are some of my favorite Bible promises in which I have placed my trust for my own personal sins and the failures in my past. God does not lie and therefore these promises are factual and always true.

Psalm 103:8-10: "The Lord is merciful and gracious, slow to anger and abounding in steadfast love. He will not always chide, nor will he keep his anger forever. He has not dealt with us according to our sins, nor repay us according to our iniquities."

Isaiah 51:12-13: "I, I am he who comforts you; who are you that you are afraid of man who dies, of the son of man who is made like grass, and have forgotten the Lord your Maker, who stretched out the Heavens and laid the foundations of the earth, and you fear continually all the day because of the wrath of the oppressor, when he sets himself to destroy?"

Psalm 103:11-14: "For as high as the heavens are above the earth, so great is his steadfast love toward those who fear him; as far as the east is from the west, so far does he remove our transgressions from us. As a father shows compassion to His children, the Lord shows compassion to those who fear him. For he knows our frame; he remembers that we are dust."

Isaiah 55:8-9: "For my thoughts are not your thoughts, neither are your ways my ways, declares the Lord. For as the heavens are higher than the earth, so are my ways higher than your ways and my thoughts than your thoughts."

Romans 5:10: "For if while we were enemies we were reconciled to God by the death of his Son, much more, now that we are reconciled, shall we be saved by his life."

Ultimately all the world suffers because of sin, even the children of pastors of churches all over America. Many a preacher's kid has turned out to be rebellious and they turn away from God. Preacher's kids (also known as PKs) suffer because they are under a higher expectation of behavior because their dad is the leader in the church.

Also the congregation often puts pressure on the pastor to bring in the numbers and the money so the pastor—a husband and a father—is never at home. He is at church putting together church services to compete with television shows. He spends long hours adding stories and jokes to his sermons to keep members in his church entertained, in order to show other pastors at annual pastors conferences that he is not a failure. In other words he is a man pleaser and not a God pleaser.

The same is true for families whose fathers are climbing the corporate ladder. This is hard on the family, and worse if both the husband and the wife work. They both fall into bed watching late night TV and miss altogether the family time, and most importantly, time spent together in the Word.

All this shows that all mankind are born sinners. Most parents struggle with parenting the willful teen or the middle school student struggling with rejection by their peers. These stories are no different than struggles of MKs—only I think it is more difficult for MKs because they are physically separated from their parents' influence for nine months out of a year.

People who suffer for whatever reason must remember that they have a God-given purpose on this earth. The main purpose is God's purpose. But people are blinded by never trusting what God is doing with the full picture of their lives. All they see are the tangled knots and threads on the backside of the tapestry. The book of Job would never have been written if he had not trusted God during the immense tragedies God put him through. Though Job would never see the full picture until Heaven, God was weaving a story for us to see that the purposes of tragedies will never be known until eternity.

Too often when tragedy strikes, people choose to not believe in a loving God. God is never absent, leaving all His creation to blunder their way through, as Deists believe.

While going through suffering, we can handle things better when we trust who God is. He is not some tiny weakling or someone who doesn't care. Following are some attributes of God, which have so much comforted me while going through such emotional pain.

First, God is always *omnipotent* (all powerful). Jeremiah 32:17, "Ah, Lord God! It is you who made the heavens and the earth by your great power and by your outstretched arm! Nothing is too hard for you."

Second, God is also *omnipresent* (everywhere all at once), which means He is everywhere at the same time. He is not out taking a walk while we are struggling on this earth. Psalm 139:7-12, "Where shall I go from your Spirit? Or where shall I flee from your presence? If I ascend to heaven you are there! If make my bed in Sheol, you are there! If I take the wings of the morning and dwell in the uttermost part of the sea, even there your hand shall lead me, and your right hand shall hold me. If I say, 'Surely darkness shall cover me and light about me be night,' even the darkness is not dark to you; the night is bright as the day for darkness is as light with you."

When being unjustly beaten and suffering torture, or bearing unfair rejection from our peers, or perhaps having heinous unbelievable atrocities inflicted upon our bodies or our spirits, we must put our trust in what the Bible says about who God is. Know also that there will come a terrible day of punishment from God to those who sin against us. Romans 12:19, "Beloved, never avenge yourselves, but leave it to the wrath of God, for it is written, 'Vengeance is mine, I will repay, says the Lord.'"

Third, God is *omniscient* (all knowing). Psalm 142:3 says "When my spirit was overwhelmed within me, then You knew my path......in which I walk." Also Psalm 103:14 "For He knows our frame: He remembers that we are dust." Psalm 139:1-5, "O Lord, you have searched me and known me! You know when I sit down and when I rise up; you discern my thoughts from afar. You searched out my path and my lying down and are acquainted with all my ways. Even before a word is on my tongue, behold, O Lord, you know it altogether. You hem me in, behind and before, and lay your hand upon me."

This is the real truth behind MKs' lives. Their suffering is the same suffering allowed by God to Christians and non-Christians all over the world.

We must know that all suffering is part of God's chosen plan and that it is for our good, though we will not know the full reason until eternity. It is God's job to bring good from our suffering.

Until we believe there's a loving God who is actively involved in this entire world, there will always be struggles against God, against His people, and against institutions and governments. The Christian is commanded to obey those in authority over us. But if one chooses to hold bitterness against God, or against certain people or institutions, that bitterness might turn to hatred and then to revenge. The Bible warns what will result if we willfully continue to sin by holding bitterness and jealousy in our hearts. James 1:14, "But each person is tempted when he is lured and enticed by his own desire. Then, desire when conceived gives birth to sin, and sin when it is fully grown brings forth death."

Back in the beginning of the Bible we have the story of the first recorded sin. "In the course of time Cain brought to the Lord an offering of the fruit of the ground, and Abel also brought of the firstborn of his flock and of the fat portions. And the Lord had regard for Abel and his offering, but for Cain and his offering he had no regard. So Cain was very angry, and his face fell. The Lord said to Cain, 'Why are you angry, and why has your face fallen? If you do well, then will you not be accepted? And if you do not well, sin is crouching at the door. Its desire is for you, but you must rule over it'" (Genesis 4:3-7). The brothers both knew that a blood sacrifice was necessary for an offering to please God. Cain willfully chose his own way to please God!

Today we see the breakdown in our society from jealousy between "the haves" and the "have-nots." For example, the Newtown shooter had been persecuted for being a have-not. He retaliated by paying people back for rejection and persecution by his peers in his childhood. Obviously this shooter was allowing dark and hateful thoughts to consume his thinking until he ultimately decided to fulfill his vengeful thoughts.

The Boston Marathon Bomber typed on his computer that he hated Americans and that they had horribly mistreated him over the years. How much of his thinking influenced his actions, in addition to his Jihadists training back in the Chechen Republic?

Why people bully another person is the question to be answered. What is the bully's purpose?

After being bullied by an ongoing tirade on

Twitter, Charlotte Dawson began an anti-bullying campaign on TV, radio, newspapers, magazines, and Twitter. Charlotte was gorgeous, successful, intelligent, and talented! Why would anyone want to bully her?

This goes back to my previous point, which is that the "have-nots" are jealous of those who "have!" They plot and work out how to bring down the one they bully because they are jealous. The jealousy urges them to cause harm to those of whom they are jealous.

If Charlotte Dawson had learned to forgive, removing any form of self-pity, prescription drugs, alcohol—and trying to use rebuttal against her accusers—she would have come out the winner! She would have been able to leave these people in the dust, forgetting, forgiving, and realizing from where her accusers were coming!

But on April 26, 2014, Charlotte Dawson, the Australian star and former model, was found dead—hanged in her gorgeous ocean view mansion.

The story of Charlotte Dawson's suicide ended with a note. In the note she wrote, "You win!" Undoubtedly she accomplished the bully's objective! She lost but they won!

Those who bully are simply jealous. They have problems! Leave them alone, forgive them, and get on with life. If you don't, and if you try to argue your case or choose not to forgive, they will bring you down! They win when you do what they do!

The Bible clearly states the cause of murders and wars in James 4:1-3, "What causes quarrels and what causes fights among you? Is it not this, that your passions are at war within you? You desire and do not have, so you murder. You covet and cannot obtain, so you fight and quarrel. You do not have, because you do not ask. You ask and do not receive, because you ask wrongly, to spend it on your passions."

The real truth about MKs is that we are sinners. The truth is that MKs must choose to believe that there is a God and He has a purpose for our trials at boarding school.

While I was in college I struggled greatly with a personal problem. I couldn't sleep at night out of fear of not being able to sleep. It caused my heart to beat wildly, keeping me awake until four in the morning. It wasn't until years later that I figured out that while cheerleading, we would drink lots of Coke. Being raised in a primitive culture I never knew that Coke had caffeine in it. I also never knew tea and hot chocolate had caffeine in it, as I had also suffered insomnia at Dalat School. So insomnia and fear would hit just when I wanted to be alert in classes and not look bad with circles under my eyes.

This fear was a nightmare. I prayed to God and searched the Bible for answers and God began to show me that He was a God of love. I searched more and more of the Bible to find my motivation to live life.

I learned that Jesus said He was God. I studied passages like John 14:9b, "Whoever has seen me has seen the Father;" also John 10:30, "I and the Father are one;" and John 1: 1-2, 14, "In the beginning was the Word and the Word was with God and the Word was God. He was in the beginning with God. And the Word became flesh and dwelt among us . . . ."

To prove Jesus is God He forgave people of their sins. God is the only one who can forgive sins. Jesus forgave sins in Mark 2:5-7, "And when Jesus saw their faith, he said to the paralytic, 'Son your sins are forgiven.' Now some of the scribes were sitting there, questioning in their hearts, 'Why does this man speak like that? He is blaspheming! Who can forgive sins but God alone?'" So Jesus was proving Himself to be God by doing something only God could do.

God IS omniscient (all-knowing). Not only does Jesus demonstrate power to forgive, He knows what people are thinking before they speak. As mentioned in the previous verses, the scribes were questioning in their minds. In the next verse, Mark 2:8, "And immediately Jesus, perceiving in his spirit that they thus questioned within themselves, said to them, 'Why do you question these things in your hearts.'"

God IS omnipotent (all-powerful). Jesus also demonstrated He was God by using supernatural power as God did. In Matthew 4:19, Jesus created bread and fish out of nothing to feed five thousand people. In Mark 4:37, Jesus had power over the wind and the sea. In verse 39, He rebuked the wind and said to the sea, "'Peace be still' and the wind ceased, and there was a great calm."

Jesus also showed His supernatural power over sicknesses. In Matthew 4:23 it says, "And he went throughout all Galilee, teaching in their synagogues and proclaiming the gospel of the kingdom and healing every disease and every affliction among the people." For example, in Matthew 20:32-34, Jesus saw two blind men, "And stopping, Jesus called them and said, 'What do you want me to do for you?' They said to him, 'Lord, let our eyes be opened.' And Jesus in pity touched their eyes, and immediately they recovered their sight and followed Him."

Death was no problem for Jesus to heal either. In Mark 7:41, Jesus brought back from the dead the synagogue ruler's daughter. In Luke 7:12, "As he drew near to the gate of the town, behold, a man who had died was being carried out, who was the only son of his mother and she was a widow." Jesus came up and just touched the stretcher and said "'Young man, I say to you, arise.' And the dead man sat up and began to speak" (vs. 14-15). Lazarus, the brother of Mary, died and was already buried for four days. In John 11:43-44, "When he had said these things, he cried out with a loud voice, 'Lazarus, come out.' The man who had died came out, his hands and feet bound with linen strips, and his face wrapped with a cloth. Jesus said to them, 'Unbind him, and let him go.'"

God has always existed and knows all the past and all the future, as told in Colossians 1:17, "And he [Jesus] is before all things, and in him all things hold together."

Jesus predicted His own suffering numerous times, such as is seen in Luke 9:22, "The Son of Man must suffer many things and be rejected by the elders and chief priests and scribes, and be killed, and on the third day rise again." Also, in Mark 8:31 and Matthew 16:21, He predicted His death and resurrection.

As I struggled with my faith, trusting God

with my insomnia, I could see that I had only three options to choose from regarding who Jesus was! First option was, maybe Jesus thought He was God but really wasn't. What would you call this person? A crazy person! The second option was, maybe Jesus knew He wasn't God but He said He was! What would you call this person? He would be called a liar. The third option was the only option that made sense because we see all throughout history institutions, governments, and leaders who used the teachings of Jesus. He has to be who He said He was—that He was God!! This fact really increased my faith in knowing there was a real living Person who loved me. I was always, from that time on, trusting and not hating because of my trials or suffering.

We own an 1885 copy of the works of Flavius Josephus, a contemporary of Jesus Christ. On the title page it says, "The Works of Josephus," and in smaller lettering it states, "with a life written by himself." Under that title it states, "Translated from the Original Greek." Below is a quote from *The Works of Josephus* VOL. II, page 148.

"Now there was about this time Jesus, a wise man, if it be lawful to call him a man; for he was a doer of wonderful works, a teacher of such men as receive the truth with pleasure. He drew over to him both many of the Jews and many Gentiles. He was the Christ. And when Pilate, at the suggestion of the principle men among us, had condemned him to the cross, those that loved him at the first did not forsake him; for he appeared to them alive again the third day; as the divine prophets had foretold these and ten thousand other wonderful things concerning him. And the tribe of Christians, so named from, are not extinct at this day."

A story is told about a man in the country of India who was a Hindu. Hindus believe that when they die their ancestors become anything from insects to a rich person, based on all the works they did in an earlier life. Suddenly, while out in the field, this Hindu man who was thinking about becoming a Christian, saw a nest of ants about twenty feet away and a stream of water was coming slowly, within 15 minutes of drowning all the ants. The Hindu man thought, "If only I could become an ant and tell them to run quickly to safety." The Hindu man knew they could escape if they would only start running fast up a nearby hill. As the man thought of this, he believed that truly God had to have become man to come down to the human level in order to explain Who God is and how to be saved from guilt and sins.

Christianity tells us what no other so-called religion tells us. Jesus did something about the guilt all humans feel. Why does every religion have to live by a code of ethics? Why were humans made to know right from wrong? Why are humans so careful to work to get to Heaven? Why are humans so consumed with the afterlife that they leave out food for the dead to eat, as do Catholics in the Philippines? The one AB-SOLUTE no one can get away from is that death will come someday.

About the time I was eight years old and and staying for vacation in Sayaboury, Laos, a neighbor's close family member died. I think it was the father. Death was so absolute that they paid the village witch doctor to be certain that the curse of death was paid for. They bought a water buffalo, which must have put them in huge debt because these people were so very poor. The witch doctor slowly killed the water buffalo, and when it died the witch doctor looked at the way the liver lay. If it was lying in a certain way then the curse of death was paid. But if not, the witch doctor would ask for another sacrifice. What I'll never forget was the loud wailing that went on all day and all night for at least three days. It was shocking to my brother and me to hear the eerie wailing and see the water buffalo slowly dying.

It is true that we all will die physically. How thankful I am to know that there is the reality of life after death. I have put my trust in the fact that, one day long ago, I asked God's Son, through His Holy Spirit to come in and give me His eternal life! 1 John 5:11-13, "And this is the testimony, that God gave us eternal life, and this life is in his Son. Whoever has the Son has life; whoever does not have the Son of God does not have life. I write these things to you who believe in the name of the Son of God that you may know that you have eternal life." In Luke 12:4-5a, Jesus is speaking and says, "I tell you my friends, do not fear those who kill the body, and after that have nothing more that they can do. But I will warn you whom to fear: fear him who has power to put you in Hell." We all sin many times and deserve Hell. We sin in thought (like jealousy or hate) and words (vengeful or thoughtless words, unintended or intended).

I noticed that during our family time reading the Bible and praying together, I felt within myself a desire to tear down my husband. I cannot remember now what I attacked my husband about (which shows how really insignificant it was at the time). I'm glad I was sensitive enough to notice this and see that I had a jealous heart! I didn't like it that he didn't seem to struggle with attitude sins like I did and this made me jealous.

At the time I realized this, I began to work hard at keeping my mouth shut and to listen, as our son Samuel, my greatest disciple, was watching. Oh how I feared that I was teaching him to be insubordinate to God. I'm so glad God showed me my heart so that I could work on keeping a right attitude by listening respectfully. God's Holy Spirit working in my heart showed me that God gave me the power to not sin by miraculously changing my heart from a jealous heart to a loving heart.

This example teaches that many are critical and unkind for the simple reason that they are jealous and wish to cause pain. I know this to be true because I wished pain on my husband simply because I was jealous that he could always forgive and be patient, no matter what suffering he was going through.

It is not that my husband did anything wrong. The problem is revealed in Genesis 4:6, that sin was lying at the door and it desired to have me. God accepted Abel's sacrifice and not Cain's. Cain was jealous. This story of Cain and Abel demonstrates to us that jealousy is most often at the root of why people reject and put us down.

People want to cause us pain because they hate us. We have something they do not have. Many things can make us jealous of others. It may be something as simple as their looks. They may be thinner than we are or have lovely eyes and beautiful hair. Or they are richer than we are. Or they are better at sports than we are. Or they are more popular then we are. Or they are smarter that we are. Or they are nicer, more forgiving, and more generous than we are.

There are other reasons why we put down people and are unkind to them. For example, irritating habits such as people who slurp their soup, or use their teeth to scrape their spoon, or who make lots of odd noises in their throat, like clearing it over and over again. Today people go in a rage over being cut in line while driving. These are people's idiosyncrasies and we need to forgive them.

Perhaps we ourselves have unknown strange ways about us that irritate others. People are patient with us—shouldn't we be patient with them? If everyone in the world acted in the same way, wouldn't the world be rather boring? The Bible says it right in Matthew 7:12, "So whatever you wish that others would do to you, do also to them, for this is the Law and the Prophets."

However this does not mean we do not protect people from needless embarrassment. The other day I noticed a white spot on my dad's dress pants. Rather than having him go around all day with this glaring spot, the most loving thing for me was to show it to him. Do you know what his response was? "Why Carolyn, I would have never known that was there. Thank you so much for pointing it out to me." His response was the right response.

When people tuck in the label hanging out of the back of your shirt, they are doing the most loving thing, and we must believe that they are showing us a kindness. Romans 12:10, "Love one another with brotherly affection. Outdo one another in showing honor."

In our need to correct others we also need to check our own motives as to why we feel the need to correct other people's faults. Ephesians 4:2b says, "bearing with one another in love." Sometimes jealousy might be the cause why people are overly critical.

True change might not come by always setting people straight whenever we see some fault in them. Not every minor fault needs to be corrected. Often God might be showing us the other person's imperfections to show us what we need to pray for, whether it be their outside dress or outward actions.

Jesus gives a perfect illustration about correcting other people's faults in Matthew 7:3-4, "Why do you see the speck that is in your brother's eye, but do not notice the log that is in your own eye? Or how can you say to your brother, 'Let me take the speck out of your eye, when there is the log in your own eye?'" We always have "logs" in our own eyes. The question is what is the log—pride about our personal knowledge, our appearance, or our accomplishments? Could the log be jealousy about how calm and well-mannered a person is, or the prestigious job another person has, or how well dressed they always are?

Often conflicts and putdowns are caused just because we have not asked God to give us what we need. James 4:1-2, "What causes quarrels and what causes fights among you? Is it not this, that your passions are at war within you? You desire and do not have, so you murder. You covet and cannot obtain, so you fight and quarrel. You do not have, because you do not ask." For example, many years ago my husband was teaching verse by verse through the book of Romans. It was as if half the church became different people when he came to the passages in Romans 3 that point to the fact that all men are sinners. They hated my husband and eventually gathered an illegal evening meeting to boot my husband out of the church. This was so painful for me to watch, but I prayed very hard for me to truly forgive and love these people. So often we do not receive because we have not asked God to give us what we need.

I asked God to help me to forgive and a miracle happened. I was able to smile and love those people who hated us so much. It was a miracle to experience the calmness and assurance I felt in answer to prayer in my own heart.

To me, my husband was a hero just like the Old Testament prophets who spoke the truth and men hated them so much they even killed some of the prophets. I was never more proud of my husband than I was at that time. He held his head high and was never ashamed of the truth of the gospel.

An amazing miracle of trust happened when I worked for a year in a hospital. My husband worked there too, but in a different department. My team's job was to physically get up and get medical charts and deliver them to their appointed destination ASAP. Whenever a call came in, I would hear, "Carolyn, you need to go get this chart." I became the brunt of jokes. The others just sat there and answered calls, when the job description was the same for all of us.

Furthermore, the man whose desk faced mine would enjoy retelling explicitly X-rated sexual scenes from movies he had seen. When he did this I never said anything but would quietly get up to find another job away from his presence. He also told me he enjoyed beating up pregnant women.

I was pregnant for eight months while working in this department. During that time I asked for Wednesdays off to get ready for our first baby. To my shock, within a day, this guy who was saying these things to me asked to be off on the same day. He knew my husband worked every day at the same hospital but in a different department. He knew I would be home alone. The back yard of our house faced miles of desolation. I prayed to God each day because I was afraid.

There were good reasons for some people to hate me because I always verbalized that I was a Christian. But always my reaction throughout the day was to ask God to help me forgive as Jesus did while He was on the Cross.

My immediate boss was a delightful English lady. During my first job review with her I handed her a gospel tract and prayed for her. Because of this, God prepared a way for me to be allowed on two occasions to share a ten minute gospel presentation with the group, on the topics of "feeling valueless" and "managing your time."

Both talks went well and so many in my department came up later to say how much they benefited from these tiny messages from the Bible. But there were four who very definitely hated me with sneers and bullying!

The Bible says in Matthew 5:11, "Blessed are you when others revile you and persecute you and utter all kinds of evil against you falsely on my account." Often people are mistreated because they act in the right way—like Christ.

We must remember that this kind of mistreatment is an honor as we are persecuted right along with such famous people as Jeremiah and Elijah. As it says in Matthew 5:12, when we are persecuted for acting right we should "Rejoice and be glad, for your reward is great in heaven, for so they persecuted the prophets who were before you."

As already mentioned, there is no human who totally loves in thought, word, and deed. The greatest command is to love God with all your heart, soul, mind and strength. And the second is to love your neighbor as yourself.

Our country needs a heart revival where forgiveness, humility, and loving kindness are the traits of every home.

One day after we had been married for about

two years, we had loaded up a U-Haul and moved all the way across the United States. I will never forget that experience and how it influenced my life. I was grumpy, complaining, and depressed, voicing my irritations. I think we had been driving for several hours and were almost in Nevada.

After all those hours of voicing my frustrations my husband calmly quoted James 1:22, "But be doers of the Word and not hearers only, deceiving your selves. For if anyone is a hearer of the Word and not a doer, he is like a man who looks at his natural face in a mirror . . . and goes away at once forgetting what he was like."

I end this book with this story because experiences we have, or knowledge of the Bible do no good if we do not apply God's Word to our lives in the midst of our suffering.

People will not see the love of Christ dwelling in us unless we have submitted ourselves by choosing by our wills to have Jesus Christ to be the King of our heart. Our wills need to be broken. We show pride when we feel wounded, when others are promoted, and when we are overlooked. Proud, unbroken people are self-conscious. They worry about what others think of them. Proud, unbroken people have a hard time saying, "I was wrong; will you please forgive me?" Proud, unbroken people have a hard time receiving criticism. Proud, unbroken people have a drive to be recognized and appreciated for their efforts.

This is why God so often has to bring trials into our life to teach humility. This is what happened in my life. Many times I see myself as having to prove that I am right and that I have to get in the last word. Also I see in my heart a craving to be noticed and to be seen as a success. I am always preoccupied with what others think and I'm always concerned about myself. I know that God may yet bring trials into my life to teach me humility. Most of our sufferings in this world would be gone if there was less of self and more of Jesus Christ's life shining brightly!

POSTSCRIPT

This book cannot be concluded without answering the question, "What would I do, if I were the missionary parent and had to make the choice to send my children away to school?"

The question may be better asked, "Is it Biblical to send children away to school?"

Missionary parents who believe it is good to send their children away to boarding school base their premise on examples of the wonderful missionaries who first began the missionary enterprise. Others have used the example of how Hannah sent her little boy of about four or five to live in the temple under the High Priest Eli without his father or mother. The quote most often used to prove that we should send our children away is from Matthew 10:37, "Whoever . . . loves his son or daughter more than me is not worthy of me."

To be perfectly honest, I'm not sure I would send my child away to boarding school if I had the choice today. We are not God. Many of the things God did in the Old Testament we may not understand, but we simply take by faith that it happened since we believe God. In Psalm 135:6, "Whatever the Lord pleases, he does, in heaven and on the earth, in the seas and all the deeps." When reading stories and historical accounts from the Bible, it is important to remember that these chapters are descriptive not prescriptive.

Jesus says in Mark 10:29-30a, " . . . There is no one who has left house or brothers or sisters or mother or father or children or lands, for my sake and for the gospel, who will not receive a hundredfold . . . ." In these verses, it is speaking about choosing to be a follower of Christ no matter what the cost. In many countries followers of Jesus count it worthy to be kicked out of their homes and rejected. These are not verses commanding parents to send their children hundreds of miles away in order that they can spread the Gospel.

But I cannot judge, because without the grace of God, there go I. I don't know for sure what I would have done fifty years ago. But looking back now, I know God wants fathers and mothers to be the primary and only nurturers and teachers of their children, helping them on a daily basis to grow up loving God with all their hearts, following the examples of their parents.

What if fifty years ago, MKs attended schools

in villages where their parent's ministry was. Perhaps because of this, doors could have been opened for their parents to have had a greater ministry in the village. What great future missionaries MKs would be!

One thing I do know is that drastic changes have been made in missions in the last forty years. God has been building His church through the lives of godly, mature indigenous people that He has raised up in every nation, tribe, and culture. Today these are the missionaries God is using to evangelize thousands in their own countries and tribal group.

God gave Dr. Finley, the founder of Christian Aid, the vision to raise funds for these godly third world indigenous men and women who are giving all their energy, life, and time to preach the gospel to their own people in every culture, country, tribe, and people group all over this world. Thousands are being saved as a result of these men of God! This is one of the most fantastic of miracles in all of history, to see these men deny riches to live in humble bamboo huts, often with leaky roofs. But they still go out every day walking or traveling remote streams to reach the people who have never heard the wonderful message of the gospel of our Lord Jesus Christ. Today it is the indigenous bondservants of God whom God is using to bring thousands into His Kingdom! All praises go to our wonderful Heavenly Father who planned this out long before the world was made! How glorious is our God! How magnificent and holy is our gracious Heavenly Father!

Brokenness Bookmark:
The Heart God Revives
by Nancy Leigh DeMoss

Proud people focus on the failures of others.
Broken people are overwhelmed with a sense of their own spiritual need.
Proud people have a critical, fault-finding spirit; they look at everyone else's faults with a microscope but their own with a telescope.
Broken people are compassionate; they can forgive much because they know how much they have been forgiven.
Proud people are self-righteous; they look down on others.
Broken people esteem all others better than themselves.
Proud people have an independent, self-sufficient spirit.
Broken people have a dependent spirit; they recognize their need for others.
Proud people have to prove that they are right.
Broken people are willing to yield the right to be right.
Proud people claim rights; they have a demanding spirit.

Broken people yield their rights; they have a meek spirit.

Proud people are self-protective of their time, their rights, and their reputation.

Broken people are self-denying.

Proud people desire to be served.

Broken people are motivated to serve others.

Proud people desire to be a success.

Broken people are motivated to be faithful and to make others a success.

Proud people desire self-advancement.

Broken people desire to promote others.

Proud people have a drive to be recognized and appreciated.

Broken people have a sense of their own unworthiness; they are thrilled that God would use them at all.

Proud people are wounded when others are promoted and they are overlooked.

Broken people are eager for others to get the credit; they rejoice when others are lifted up.

Proud people have a subconscious feeling, "This ministry/church is privileged to have me and my gifts"; they think of what they can do for God.

Broken people's heart attitude is, "I don't deserve to have a part in any ministry"; they know that they have nothing to offer God except the life of Jesus flowing through their broken lives.

Proud people feel confident in how much they know.

Broken people are humbled by how very much they have to learn.

Proud people are self-conscious.

Broken people are not concerned with self at all.

Proud people keep others at arms' length.

Broken people are willing to risk getting close to others and to take risks of loving intimately.

Proud people are quick to blame others.

Broken people accept personal responsibility and can see where they are wrong in a situation.

Proud people are unapproachable or defensive when criticized.

Broken people receive criticism with a humble, open spirit.

Proud people are concerned with being respectable, with what others think; they work to protect their own image and reputation.

Broken people are concerned with being real; what matters to them is not what others think but what God knows; they are willing to die to their own reputation.

Proud people find it difficult to share their spiritual need with others.

Broken people are willing to be open and transparent with others as God directs.

Proud people want to be sure that no one finds out when they have sinned; their instinct is to cover up.

Broken people, once broken, don't care who knows or who finds out; they are willing to be exposed because they have nothing to lose.

Proud people have a hard time saying, "I was wrong; will you please forgive me?"

Broken people are quick to admit failure and to seek forgiveness when necessary.

Proud people tend to deal in generalities when confessing sin.

Broken people are able to acknowledge specifics

when confessing their sin.

Proud people are concerned about the consequences of their sin.

Broken people are grieved over the cause, the root of their sin.

Proud people are remorseful over their sin, sorry that they got found out or caught.

Broken people are truly, genuinely repentant over their sin, evidenced in the fact that they forsake that sin.

Proud people wait for the other to come and ask forgiveness when there is a misunderstanding or conflict in a relationship.

Broken people take the initiative to be reconciled when there is misunderstanding or conflict in relationships; they race to the cross; they see if they can get there first, no matter how wrong the other may have been.

Proud people compare themselves with others and feel worthy of honor.

Broken people compare themselves to the holiness of God and feel a desperate need for His mercy.

Proud people are blind to their true heart condition.

Broken people walk in the light.

Proud people don't think they have anything to repent of.

Broken people realize they have need of a continual heart attitude of repentance.

Proud people don't think they need revival, but they are sure that everyone else does.

Broken people continually sense their need for a fresh encounter with God and for a fresh filling of His Holy Spirit.

© Revive Our Hearts.

https://www.reviveourhearts.com/articles/bro-

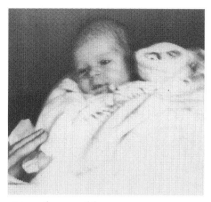

Seven hours old.

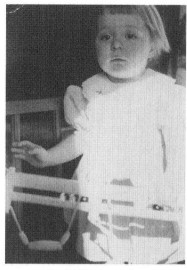

One and a half years old.

Cradle my father made for me for my second birthday.

The porch where I found the King Cobra snake.

Family picture taken in 1952.

Best friends, Paul.

Pulling Paul in the wagon my father made.

Talking with the chickens with my brother Paul.

My real live baby doll gibbon.

Visiting neighbors across the street.

Chapel on the left and my home on the right.

Lookng out my bedroom window.

Working in my dad's garden.

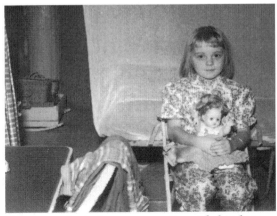

No screened windows—mosquito net behind me.

172

Saying goodbye to my dad as he goes on a mission trip.

Elephant in front of our house in Sayaboury.

My mother and the Jeep parked next to our next door neighbor.

My mother and the water tanks we played on.

Going to school for the first time.

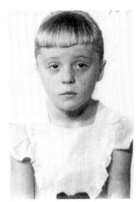

1957.

Dalat School Vietnam.

Some of my roommates.

174

Third grade—front row, third from right.

Fourth grade—far left front row.

Fifth grade—sitting far upper right.

175

Weekly laundry—fifth grade.

Sixth grade.

Picnic at volcanic rocks—seventh grade.

Picnic in yard—food cooked in foil buried underground on coals.

176

Flying airplanes with my brothers.

Tribal Christmas dinner.

Ninth grade.

Eighth grade on furlough.

177

Tenth grade.

Tenth grade with Paul and his friend.

MKs from Laos—eleventh grade.

1969 Dalat graduating class in Tanah Rata, Malaysia.

High school graduation.

Senior Sneak—guys throwing me up in the air.

Dear Grandma Tubbs   Nov 7 1962
    Thank you so much for the letter. It
arrived the 3rd

        How is everything there. You know
were praying for you

        Say hi to everbody there

        David brought a dog down from
Dallas. It is brown with a little black
here and there his tail is all black, too.
We call him Tipper

        Paul and Me are so excited for
Christmase that were allready playing
christmase records on the record player
We allways wonder what were going to
get
            Love carolyn
                    Joyce
        X X X X X   Tubbs
        O O O O O

Letter written to Grandmother Tubbs, November 7, 1962.

180

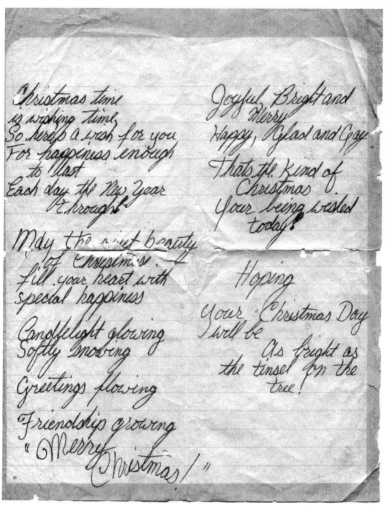

Christmas time
is wishing time,
So here's a wish for you
For happiness enough
to last
Each day the New Year
through!

May the quiet beauty
of Christmas
fill your heart with
special happiness

Candlelight glowing
Softly snowing
Greetings flowing
Friendship growing
"Merry Christmas!"

Joyful, Bright and
Merry
Happy, Glad and Gay
That's the Kind of
Christmas
Your being wished
today!

Hoping
Your Christmas Day
will be
As bright as
the tinsel on the
tree!

Letter written to Grandmother.

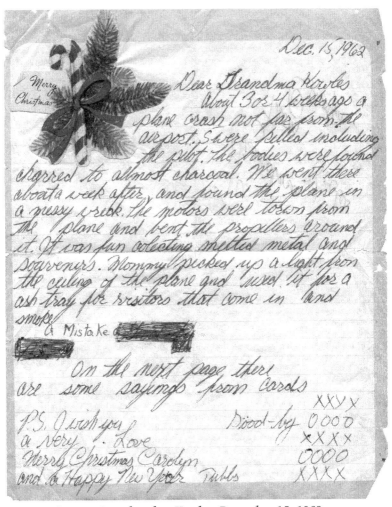

Dec. 15, 1962

Merry
Christmas

Dear Grandma Kowles
About 3 or 4 weeks ago a plane crash not far from the airport. 5 were killed including the pilot. The bodies were found charred to almost charcoal. We went there about a week after, and found the plane in a messy wreck. The motors were torn from the plane and bent the propellers around it. It was fun collecting melted metal and souvenirs. Mommy picked up a light from the ceiling of the plane and used it for a ash tray for visitors that come in and smoke.

a Mistake

On the next page there are some sayings from cards

P.S. I wish you a very
Merry Christmas
and a Happy New Year

Love
Carolyn
Tubbs

Dood-by

XXYX
OOOO
XXXX
OOOO
XXXX

Letter written to Grandmother Kowles, December 15, 1962.

182

41364047R00105

Made in the USA
Lexington, KY
10 May 2015